主　编：张 黎
Chief Editor：Zhang Li

商务汉语系列教材
Business Chinese Readers

(1)

商务汉语入门——基本礼仪篇

Gateway to Business Chinese
Regular Formulas and Etiquette

编著：沈庶英
Compiler：Shen Shuying
英文翻译：熊文华
English Translator：Xiong Wenhua

图书在版编目(CIP)数据

商务汉语入门——基本礼仪篇/张黎主编. —北京：北京大学出版社，2005.4
(商务汉语系列教材)
ISBN 978-7-301-08541-7

Ⅰ.商… Ⅱ.张… Ⅲ.商务-汉语-对外汉语教学-教材 Ⅳ.H195.4

中国版本图书馆 CIP 数据核字（2005）第 141540 号

书　　名：商务汉语入门——基本礼仪篇
著作责任者：张　黎　主编　沈庶英　编著
英 文 翻 译：熊文华
责 任 编 辑：邓晓霞　dxxvip@vip.sina.com
封 面 设 计：张婷婷
标 准 书 号：ISBN 978-7-301-08541-7/H · 1395
出 版 发 行：北京大学出版社
地　　址：北京市海淀区成府路 205 号　100871
网　　址：http://www.pup.cn
电 子 信 箱：zpup@pup.pku.edu.cn
电　　话：邮购部 62752015　发行部 62750672　出版部 62754962　编辑部 62752028
排 版 者：国美嘉誉文化艺术有限公司
印 刷 者：北京中科印刷有限公司
图片提供者：和滨视讯传媒技术（北京）有限公司
经 销 者：新华书店
787 毫米×1092 毫米　16 开本　13.25 印张　300 千字
2005 年 4 月第 1 版　2010 年 6 月第 5 次印刷
印　　数：14001～17000 册
定　　价：48.00 元（附 1 张 MP3）

《商务汉语》系列教材编写说明

编写目的

随着中国的发展，中国与世界各国，尤其是与发达国家之间的交往、贸易以及商务活动越来越多，从而推动了外国人学习中文的热潮。据调查，全球已有超过100个国家开设汉语教学课程，学习汉语的人数达到3000万人，有12400余所各级各类学校开设汉语课程，在学学生达330多万人。2003年全球参加汉语水平考试的考生人数达30万人，创历史新高。而学习汉语的人当中，很多人是为了与中国做生意或在与中国有关系的公司中工作，中国经济的飞速发展为全世界提供了巨大的商机，外国企业纷纷到中国寻求发展机会。同时，随着中国成为“世界工厂”，十几万外国企业落户中国，几十万外国企业家和经营管理人员在中国工作。以上这些人都有掌握一些用汉语交际的能力的需求，以满足商业交往与沟通的需要。为此，在中国国家对外汉语教学领导小组办公室的支持下，我们编写了这套《商务汉语系列教材》。

适用对象

想学习汉语的工商界人士中，很少有人能够抽出一段相对集中的时间去学校系统地学习汉语课程，他们大多只能在有限的业余时间内参加速成班、进行个别教学或者自学。他们不是把汉语作为学校里的专业去学习，并不期望系统地掌握非常流利的汉语，而是希望学习与商务往来有关的一些实用的基本语言知识和技能，以便能够克服商务活动中的基本语言障碍，改善与中国人沟通的效果，增加成功的机会。本教材就是针对这些人的特殊需求编写，适用于完全没有或只具有一点汉语基础的、母语为汉语以外的语言的工商界人士以及其他希望学习一些基础商务汉语的人。

技能目标

中外经济、商务交往，本质上是一种跨文化的交际行为。为了商业的成功，首先必须消除作为交际工具的语言方面的障碍，其次要消除文化的障碍，理解和掌握目的语所代表的文化、特点和规则，所以外国人学习商务汉语要获得的能力包含三个方面：

（1）与商务活动相关的、实用的、基本的汉语语言知识和技能。

（2）在中国经济环境下开展商务交际的能力，需要掌握基本的中国经济环境的特点、经济活动规则，既应包括贸易、投资、合作的方面的交际能力，也应包括企业管理方面的交际能力。

(3) 在中外经济交流与合作的背景下的跨文化交际能力，包括商务礼俗、惯例和中国文化背景知识。

因此，商务汉语教学应该是以语言为载体、结合商务活动和跨文化认知的三位一体的能力培养。这种能力体现在语言交际技能上，可以划分由低到高的4个层次：

(1) 必要的礼节性交际技能，如欢迎、问候、介绍、道歉、祝贺等。

(2) 实用日常交际技能，如购物、旅行、乘车、通信、约见等。

(3) 基本商务信息交流技能，如介绍公司、说明产品、询价、报价、征询意见、陈述意见等。

(4) 一定的协商、洽谈技能，如讨价还价、制定与修改计划、讨论合作方式、事物评价、问题分析、解决纠纷等。

这套《商务汉语》系列教材就是系统地训练学习者掌握以上4个层次的基本技能。完成全部教材的学习，学习者可以掌握汉语的语音、基本语法、200多个常用的口语句型、1200个左右的词汇、500多个汉字。学习者根据自己的需要确定整体学习目标或阶段目标，选择学习到哪一层次。

汉字对于外国人来说是学习的一大难点，本教材中的汉字只作为辅助的教学内容，学习者可以自己选择学习汉字与否。

教学内容

以对华商务活动为背景，以交际功能为纲组织语言项目，重在口语会话。具体包括以下几方面内容：

(1) 汉语商务交际表达话语：以各种交际功能的汉语单句为主要教学内容，在提高和强化阶段适当引入常用的复句组合。

(2) 常用商务和日常基本词汇：与会话教学相结合讲授，并适当加以扩展。

(3) 语音：以汉语拼音为载体，针对所给出的词汇，循序渐进讲授和练习汉语的发音。

(4) 汉字：通过展示和适当的讲解，让学习者可以认识最常用的汉字，不要求会写；根据具体情况，学习者也可以选择不学习汉字。

(5) 课文和生词的英文翻译、语音、语法的英文讲解。

(6) 练习：进行语音、词汇和会话训练，以加强理解、熟练掌握。

(7) 文化背景知识：系统地穿插中国社会文化、风俗习惯以及商务文化背景知识的介绍。

教学方法

(1) 本教材采用印刷文本和多媒体材料相结合的方式，学习者和教师可以充分

地利用多媒体材料进行学习和教学。

(2) 每个教学单元以交际功能为单位组织练习，在典型和常用交际场景中学习和练习完成交际技能的语言知识和技能。

(3) 利用本教材既可以进行多人集中授课的课堂教学，也可以用于个别辅导教学，还可用于自学。

教材构成

商务汉语教材共有三册：

(1)《商务汉语入门》(基本礼节篇) 针对初学者，训练必要的商务与日常礼节性交际语言技能；

(2)《商务汉语入门》(日常交际篇) 针对初学者，训练实用基本生活交际语言技能；

(3)《商务汉语提高》(应酬篇、办公篇、业务篇) 针对已经掌握一点简单汉语的学习者，训练基本商务信息交流语言交际技能。

上述三部分既是水平由低到高的系列，同时也体现对商务汉语交际功能的不同需求类型，具有相对的独立性。学习者根据自己的情况，可以成系列地学习，也可以选择其中的一本或两本学习。其中的《商务汉语提高》不是其前部分的低难度的提高和教学内容的扩大，而注重对已有汉语知识和能力的巩固、熟练和融会贯通。一方面，前面所学的语言项目会在后面的教材中重现，强化记忆，提高熟练程度；另一方面，语言项目复现的场景、功能会有所扩展，语境和句法组合方式也更加丰富，这可以使读者对已有语言知识扩展、加深，能更广泛、更准确地使用。

本教材配有多媒体资料，三册各配有一张多媒体光盘。

关于作者

《商务汉语》系列教材由中国北京语言大学经贸汉语系具有丰富商务汉语教学经验的教师编写，具体人员如下：

主编：张黎

中文作者：沈庶英：《商务汉语入门》(基本礼节篇)

聂学慧：《商务汉语入门》(日常交际篇)

陶晓红：《商务汉语提高》(应酬篇、办公篇、业务篇)

英文作者：熊文华

英文审校：Paul Denman (英国)

作者电子邮箱：jmx02@blcu.edu.cn

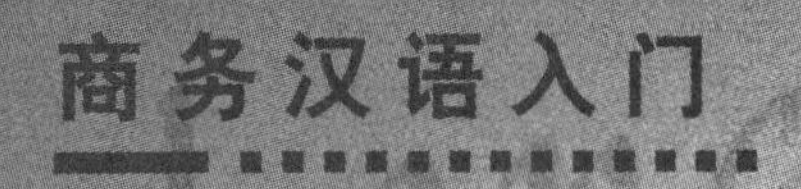

A Description of Business Chinese Readers

Compilers' Aims

Recent developments in China help accelerate her links with foreign countries, especially with the developed countries, by increasing exchange of visits and business. As a happy result a good number of foreigners take great interest in learning Chinese. It is reported that Chinese is taught to 30 million students in more than 100 countries in the world; that over 3.3 million students are taking Chinese courses at various levels in over 12,400 institutions and schools. In the year of 2003 alone the number of foreign participants in HSK (Chinese Proficiency Test) reached to 300,000, the greatest number registered ever before. A large number of the learners are believed to be those people who wish to do business with China or work for the companies which have close contact with their Chinese counterparts. China's speedy economic progress has opened up a new vista of commercial opportunities that no foreign companies can afford to lose. Modern China has been regarded as a "World Factory" where over one hundred thousand foreign enterprises have settled down, and hundreds of thousand foreign entrepreneurs, businessmen and managers are living and working. They are very much eager to learn Chinese as their tool of daily communication with the native people, and have commercial contact with local dealers. Programmed and supported by China National Office For Teaching Chinese as a Foreign Language (NOCFL), we, the members of the Compiling Group, have prepared *Business Chinese Readers*.

For Whom the Course is Intended

Among the industrialists and businessmen who wish to learn Chinese there is nearly no one who is able to take a systematic course at an institution. The great majority of them would like to take a part-time short course, self-taught or person-to-person lessons instead, because they do not want to take Chinese as their major, nor do they wish to become a fluent speaker of Chinese. All they wish to do is to acquire necessary Chinese knowledge and skills that may be needed in their communication with Chinese people without too much difficulty, and thus to enhance their success in business. The present course is prepared for those industrialists and businessmen who have never learned or have just begun learning basic Chinese that is not their mother tongue.

Skills to be Taught

Any economic and commercial transaction between China and a foreign country may be viewed as cross-cultural activities in nature. The removal of language barriers and difficulties that lie in the understanding of the culture, subtle points and principles expressed by a target

language will be greatly beneficial for one's commercial success. It is advisable, therefore, for foreigners to acquire the following abilities through learning a textbook of business Chinese:

(1) Basic Chinese knowledge and skills that is applicable to one's commercial activities;

(2) Communicative ability appropriate to Chinese environment ----- be able to understand the essentials of Chinese economic circumstances and rules for business performance, including trade, investment, cooperation and management of enterprises;

(3) Competence for cross-cultural communication in the context of economic and cooperative interchange ----- a wide range of knowledge of business custom and rules in addition to the background information of Chinese culture.

Therefore it seems appropriate to design the teaching of business Chinese in three-in-one training pattern that combines the language as a carrier with commercial activities and cross-cultural knowledge. Such skills to be used in language communication may be provided at four levels in an ascending order:

(1) Ability to use appropriate expressions on polite social occasion of reception, greeting, introduction, apology and congratulation.

(2) Ability to use appropriate expressions for shopping, traveling, bus riding, telephoning and appointment making.

(3) Ability to use appropriate expressions for commercial activities such as giving a brief account of a company or product, getting or giving a quotation, comment or statement.

(4) Ability to use appropriate expressions in consulting, negotiating, bargaining, writing or revising a plan, discussing a way to cooperate, making a comment on a subject in addition to analyzing and sorting out problems.

The present *Business Chinese Readers* aim at helping learners to acquire the 4-level ability described above. By completing this course they will have learned Chinese phonetics, basic Chinese grammar, over 200 commonly used sentence patterns, about 1200 words and 500 Chinese characters. Learners may make an overall plan of their own, or decide what stage of the three that they are going to reach.

Chinese characters may be difficult for some learners, but they only function as a supplementary tool in learning this course. Learners will decide for themselves to learn them or not.

Contents Applicable to Teaching

In each text of the book the language items are organized in a conversation on the basis of communicative function against a commercial Chinese background. Precisely they are ---

(1) Commercial Chinese expressions: Simple sentences are grouped together according to their correlative function. Useful compound sentences would not be introduced until they reach the advance and intensive stage.

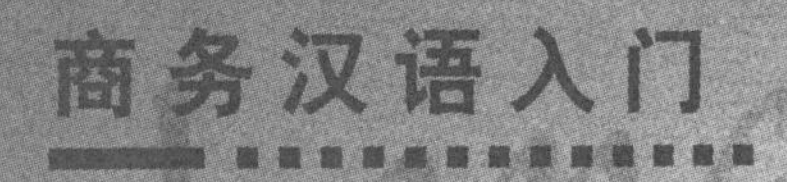

(2) A commonly-used basic commercial vocabulary: It is provided alongside with each classroom conversation and its expansion.

(3) Pronunciation: *Pinyin* is taught as an instrument for phonetics in the process of learning Chinese words and expressions.

(4) Chinese characters: By following well-illustrated explanations learners will be able to recognize commonly-used Chinese characters. They may have a choice in learning or not learning to write them.

(5) English explanation is given to each text, new words, grammar items and phonetics.

(6) Exercises: Phonetic, lexical and conversational exercises are designed for learners to fully comprehend and familiarize themselves with the texts.

(7) Cultural background knowledge: Inserted in between are the brief accounts of Chinese society, culture, customs and commercial background knowledge.

Teaching Methodology

(1) This course provides printed textbooks accompanied by multimedia discs. Teachers and learners may avail themselves of both to get the best expected.

(2) Practice and drills are arranged for each unit classified by various communicative function. In typical and common situations learners are given necessary knowledge and skills for communication.

(3) Learners may go to a class for group tuition or take private lessons under a tutor, or even learn self-taught lessons provided by the course book.

The Organization of the Constituent Volumes

Business Chinese Readers consist of three volumes:

(1) *Gateway to Business Chinese* (Regular Formulas And Etiquette) is designed for beginners learning necessary Chinese expressions for daily commercial communication and skills for polite social intercourse.

(2) *Gateway to Business Chinese* (Daily Communication) is prepared for beginners who acquire language skills in day-to-day social dealings.

(3) *Advanced Business Chinese* (Social Gatherings, Office Work, Day-To-Day Operations) is devised for the training of intermediate learners in language skills for business information exchange.

The ascending three-stage arrangement of the textbooks will meet different needs and each one may stand by itself. Learners have a free choice in taking the course as a whole or just follow one or two parts of it. The third volume does not simply serve as an advanced textbook in terms of difficulty or expansion. What's important is that they focus on the consolidation,

proficiency and mastery of the Chinese knowledge acquired through a comprehensive study of the subject. The repetition of the language items is beneficial for learners to memorize and employ them well, and the reoccurrence of the dialogue situations will be good for the repeated use of the expressions and the introduction of new contextual and syntactic formation. By so doing learners will be able to understand and apply what they have learned in a better, wider and more precise manner.

Each of the volumes is accompanied with a CD for multimedia use.

Co-Authors

Business Chinese Readers have been prepared by a group of teachers experienced in business Chinese teaching. They are---

Chief Editor: Zhang Li

Chinese Co-Authors: Shen Shuying, writer of *Gateway to Business Chinese* (Regular Formulas And Etiquette) ;
Nie Xuehui, writer of *Gateway to Business Chinese* (Daily Communication);
Tao Xiaohong, writer of *Advanced Business Chinese* (Social Gatherings, Office Work, Day-To-Day Operations)

English Co-Author: Xiong Wenhua

English Reviser: Paul Denman (Britain)

Our E-Mail Address: jmx02@blcu.edu.cn

附表 A List of Useful Terms

汉语词类表 Chinese Parts of Speech

词 类 Parts of Speech	拼 音 *Pinyin*	简 称 Abbreviation	英 译 English
名 词	míngcí	名 *n.*	noun
专有名词	zhuāngyǒu míngcí	专名 *pn.*	proper noun
数 词	shùcí	数 *num.*	numeral
量 词	liàngcí	量 *mw.*	measure word
动 词	dòngcí	动 *v.*	verb
形容词	xíngróngcí	形 *adj.*	adjective
代 词	dàicí	代 *pron.*	pronoun
副 词	fùcí	副 *adv.*	adverb
介 词	jiècí	介 *prep.*	preposition
连 词	liáncí	连 *conj.*	conjunction
助 词	zhùcí	助 *aux.*	auxiliary word
叹 词	tàncí	叹 *int.*	Interjection
语气词	yǔqìcí	语气 *mp.*	modal particle

汉语句子的主要成分 Main Constituents of Chinese Sentences

名称 Constituents	拼音 *Pinyin*	英译 English
主 语	zhǔyǔ	subject
谓 语	wèiyǔ	predicate
宾 语	bīnyǔ	object
定 语	dìngyǔ	adjective modifier
状 语	zhuàngyǔ	adverbial modifier
补 语	bǔyǔ	complement

目 录

Contents

Dì-yī kè Yǔyīn
第 1 课 语音
Lesson 1 Phonetics

导学 Guiding Remarks

现在我们开始学习汉语的发音。

汉语的语音系统中，音素是最小的语音片段，可分为元音、辅音两大类。汉语的声母和韵母就是由音素构成的。音节是语音的基本结构单位，是由一个或几个音素组成。汉语的书写符号是汉字，一般来说每个汉字的读音就是一个音节。但是汉字不是纯粹的表音文字，为了方便学习汉语和认读汉字，中国设计了一套注音符号，用来标注汉字的发音，这套符号叫做汉语拼音。汉语拼音符号都是采用的跟英语一样的拉丁字母，但实际发音与英语字母的发音大部分都不同，在学习时要注意二者的区别。

To begin with, we'll learn how to utter the Chinese sounds.

Syllables composed of vowels and consonants are the smallest units in the Chinese phonetic system. Initials and vowels are formed with syllables. A character, the written form of the Chinese language, stands for a syllable. But Chinese is not a truly phonetic language. To help learners read Chinese characters a *pinyin* system has been designed for transliterating them into a phonetic alphabet. The letters thus adopted are identical to the English ones, but they are not phonetically equal to each other. Therefore it is advisable for learners to take note of the difference between them.

汉语的音节由声母、韵母和声调构成。声母是一个音节的开头的部分，基本都是辅音；韵母是在声母后面的部分，由元音或元音和辅音的组合构成；声调是音节音高的变化。

A Chinese syllable is composed of an initial that forms its beginning part, and a final that covers its remainder, in addition to a tone mark that indicates a variation of speech pitch. Most of the initials are consonants, and the finals consist of the vowels or is the combination of vowels and consonant.

一、声母 Initials

声母有 21 个：

There are 21 initials in Chinese:

b p m f d t n l g k h j q x zh ch sh r z c s

声母的发音方法：

Ways of pronouncing the initials:

1. 发 b p 时，上下唇紧闭阻住气流，气流冲破阻碍发出声音。
   "b" and "p" are pronounced by a puff of breath stopped by the tightly closing lips then let off from them.

2. 发 m 时，上下唇紧闭阻住气流，气流从鼻腔中出来发出声音。
   "m" is formed by sending out air through the nasal cavity with tightly closing lips.

3. 发 f 时，上齿和下唇靠近，气流从缝隙中挤出发出声音。
   "f" occurs when the air is squeezed out through the air-passage narrowed between the lower lip and the upper teeth.

4. 发 d t 时，舌尖放在上齿龈上阻住气流，气流冲破阻碍发出声音。
   "d" and "t" are pronounced with the breath of air stopped by the tip of the tongue against the upper teeth gum and then let off.

5. 发 n 时，舌尖放在上齿龈阻住气流，气流从鼻腔中出来发出声音。
   "n" is given by letting the air out of the nasal cavity with the tip of the tongue against the upper teeth gum.

6. 发 l 时，舌尖放在上腭上，气流从舌头两边流出发出声音。
   "l" is pronounced by the air from both sides of the tongue with its tip touching the upper palate.

7. 发 g k 时，舌面后部放在软腭上阻住气流，气流冲破阻碍发出声音。
   "g" and "k" are pronounced by the air puffed out with the back of the tongue against the soft palate.

8. 发 h 时，舌面后部靠近软腭，气流从缝隙中挤出发出声音。

"h" is uttered by squeezing out the air with the back of the tongue close to the soft palate.

9.发 j q 时，舌面前部放在硬腭上阻住气流，慢慢让气流从缝隙中挤出发出声音。
"j" and "q" are uttered with a slow breath of air from the narrow passage formed by the front of the tongue and the hard palate.

10.发 x 时，舌面前部靠近硬腭，气流从缝隙中挤出发出声音。
"x" is made by the air squeezed out with the front of the tongue close to the hard palate.

11.发 zh ch 时，舌尖放在硬腭上阻住气流，慢慢让气流从缝隙中挤出发出声音。
"zh" and "ch" are articulated with slow breath of air squeezed out from a narrow opening between the tongue-tip and the hard palate.

12.发 sh r 时，舌尖和硬腭靠紧，气流从缝隙中挤出发出声音。
"sh" and "r" are pronounced by allowing the air to be squeezed out with the tongue-tip raising to the hard palate.

13.发 z c 时，舌尖放在上齿背上阻住气流，慢慢让气流从缝隙中挤出发出声音。
"z" and "c" are pronounced when the slow movement of air is made through the narrow passage formed by the tongue-tip against the back of the upper teeth.

14.发 s 时，舌尖和上齿背靠近，气流从缝隙中挤出发出声音。
"s" is pronounced by allowing the breath of air to squeeze out from the narrow passage with the tongue-tip raising to the back of the upper teeth.

注意：Points to be noted:

(1) "zh ch sh" 和 "z c s" 发音的区别
The differences between the articulation of "zh", "ch", "sh" and that of "z", "c", "s":

发 z c s 时，舌尖是平的，发 zh ch sh 时舌尖是卷起的。
"z", "c" and "s" are pronounced with a flat tongue-tip whereas the articulation of "zh", "ch" and "sh" is made by curling the tip of the tongue.

(2) b/p d/t g/k z/c zh/ch j/q 的区别
The differences between "b" and "p", "d" and "t", "g" and "k", "z" and "c", "zh" and "ch", "j" and "q":

汉语的声母中有送气音和不送气音的区别。p、t、k、c、ch、q 是送气音，b、d、g、z、zh、j 是不送气音。发音时请在你的嘴前面放一张薄纸，发送气音 p、t、k、c、ch、q 时，纸动了，你就发对了；相反，发不送气音 b、d、g、z、 zh、j时，纸不动，你就发对了。

The Chinese aspirated "p", "t", "k", "c", "ch" and "q" are different from the unaspirated "b", "d", "g", "z", "zh" and "j" in the tongue positions. Your correct pronunciation of the aspirated sounds of "p", "t", "k", "c", "ch" and "q" may be verified by the vibration of a piece of paper piece before your mouth in the utterance of them. On the other hand, no puffing is detected with such paper before the mouth when the unaspirated sounds of "b", "d", "g", "z", "zh" and "j" are pronounced.

(3) 汉语辅音没有清浊的对立，b、d、g三个音的发音部位跟英语基本相同，但发音时声带不振动，注意不要发成英语的浊辅音。

There are no corresponding pairs of voiced and voiceless Chinese consonants. "b","d" and"g"are almost equal to their corresponding English sounds in terms of their articulated tongue positions, but the vocal cords do not vibrate when the Chinese consonants are pronounced. Be sure not to confuse them.

二、韵母 Finals

韵母有35个,见下表:

There are 35 Chinese finals given below:

——	i	u	ü
a	ia	ua	——
o	——	uo	——
e	ie	——	üe
ai	——	uai	——
ei	——	uei	——
ao	iao	——	——
ou	iou	——	——
an	ian	uan	üan
en	in	uen	ün
ang	iang	uang	——
eng	ing	ueng	——
ong	iong	——	——

三、声调 Tones

汉语的声调有区别意义的作用，汉语的基本声调有四个，分别为阴平、阳平、上升、去声，也叫做一声、二声、三声、四声，分别用"ˉ ˊ ˇ ˋ"符号表示，标注在音节中的元音字母上面。如果在一个音节中同时有两个以上元音字母，声调就标注在主要元音上面。元音从主到次是按a、o、e、i、u、ü的顺序排列的。汉语的四个声调读起来有点像唱歌。以"a"为例，打电话时，当听

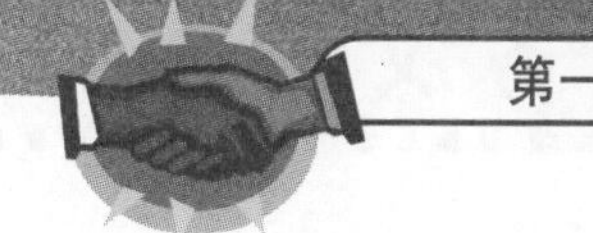

对方说话时，常常发出“ā”的应答声，“ā”表示自己在听；当听到不明白的地方，或有不同意见时，发出反问“á”声，“á？你说什么？”表示疑问；当经过对方的解释后明白了，就会发出“ǎ”声，“ǎ，是这样啊。”表示已经了解；当表示赞同对方的意见时，就会说“à，对对。”表示同意。

Chinese tones are used to differentiate meanings. There are four basic tones known as the flat tone, the rising tone, the rising tone, and the falling tone, or the first tone, the second tone, the third tone and the fourth tone, respectively represented by the pitch-graphs “ˉ”, “ˊ”, “ˇ” and “ˋ” on the vowels of a syllable such as “a”, “o”, “e”, “i”, “u”, “ü. If there were two or more vowels in a syllable, the mark would be labeled on the main vowel. The tones are uttered in a singing manner. For example, “ā” is given as the indication of one's response in a telephone conversation, “á” often shows one's doubt or disagreement, “ǎ” represents one's understanding after necessary explanation, and “à” is used to express one's approval.

汉语的声调很有意思，如果你一时还不能掌握，不要着急，慢慢来。等你学会了它，你会对汉语更有兴趣的。相信你一定行。

The Chinese tones are interesting for you to learn. Take it easy when you are unable to grasp them at first. Believe it or not, once you have mastered them, you'll feel much more eager about learning Chinese. You can surely do it.

四、拼合规则 Rules of Phonetic Spelling

i 行韵母前面没有声母时写做 yi ya ye yao you yan yin yang ying yong。

In the column i : When preceded by no initial, the finals are written as yi, ya, ye, yao, you, yan, yin, yang, ying or yong.

u 行韵母前面没有声母的时候写做 wu wa wo wai wei wan wen wang weng。

In the column u: When preceded by no initial, the finals are written as wu, wa, wo, wai, wei, wan, wen, wang or weng.

ü 行韵母前面没有声母的时候写做 yu yue yuan yun，ü 上两点省掉。

In the column ü : When preceded by no initial, the finals are written as yu, yue, yuan or yun without two dots above “ü”.

ü 行韵母跟 j q x 相拼的时候 ü 上两点省掉，写做 ju，qu，xu；juan，quan，xuan；jue，que，xue；jun，qun，xun.跟 n l 相拼时写做 nü lü，ü 上两点不省掉。

In the column ü : When going with “j”, “q” or “x” the final “ü” is written without two dots above such as in ju, qu, xu; juan, quan, xuan; jue, que, xue; jun, qun, xun. But the two dots remain unchanged when “ü” is written with “n” and “l”.

j q x 与 u 不能相拼。

The initials “j”, “q” and “x” are never used with “u”.

iou uei uen 前面加声母时写做 iu ui un。

When preceded by an initial, “iou”, “uei” and “uen” are reduced to “iu”, “ui” and “un” in their respective writing.

练习 Exercises

1. 点击跟读声母。
Double click the "initial" button and read the initials after the demonstration.

2. 点击跟读韵母。
Double click the "final" button and read the finals after the demonstration.

3. 点击音节，注意声调。
Double click the "syllable" button and focus your attention on the tone given.

4. 点击音节拼合总表，跟读整体音节。
Double click the "combination table" button and read the syllables after the demonstration.

5. 点击光盘，比较zh ch sh和z c s发音的不同。
Open the CD, click the "initial" button, and compare the pronunciation of "zh","ch" and "sh" with that of "z", "c" and "s".

6. 点击光盘，注意ü的发音。
Open the CD, click the "final" button and see how "ü" is pronounced.

7. 自己发一个音，试着拼一拼。
Try to pronounce a Chinese speech sound and write it down in phonetic alphabet.

Dì-èr kè　Nǐ hǎo
第2课　你好
Lesson 2　Hello

导学 Guiding Remarks

从今天起你就开始学说中国话了，在学习之前，让我们先一起来认识一下本书中的几个主要人物。这是Michael Black（图1），美国BM化妆品公司中国分公司总经理，中国同事和朋友亲切地称呼他“麦克（Mike）”或“麦总”；这是李琳（图2），该公司总经理助理。还有三位经常出现的人物：王光（图3），该公司销售部经理；John Smith（图4），BM美国公司的技术指导；刘力（图5），BM公司的客户，长期合作伙伴。本书主要是围绕着这几个人在中国的商务活动和生活场景展开的一些交际活动。其实他们的这些活动，你在中国也会遇到，那么现在就请你和他们一起说吧，只要他们怎么说你就怎么说，你就会很快学会中国话的，那样会给你在中国的生活和工作带来很大的方便。

我们先从打招呼开始。HELLO中国人怎么说呢，今天我们就来介绍一下。学习了本课后，当你再见到中国人的时候，看看你能不能也用汉语HELLO一下。如果你能够准确说出，你就开始像一个中国人了，你还可以让你的中国朋友大吃一惊，并且对你刮目相看了。

From today onwards you are going to learn spoken Chinese. Let's meet our characters before you learn about them from the textbook. This is Michael Black, the General Manager of the China Branch of the American BM Cosmetics Company. He is called Mike or Maizong—a term of endearment by his Chinese colleagues and friends. And here is Li Lin, the assistant to the General Manager. There are three more people we'll meet time and again in the book. They are: the sales manager Wang Guang, the Technical Adviser John Smith and their longtime partner and customer Liu Li. The present textbook is about their business routine, social communication and daily life in China. You are likely to encounter such people and be involved in similar business dealings in China. Would you like to join them in learning spoken Chinese? Just repeat what they say, and you'll be able to speak Chinese well. Surely the planned lessons will be of great benefit to you and help you live and work here.

Our first topic is to say hello. What's the Chinese for it? Well, I'm going to explain them to you. It is advisable to use the expressions after you have learned them. You'll become a true member of the Chinese community with the correct use of Chinese greetings that will give your Chinese friends a happy surprise.

A

Everybody says "Good morning" to Mike who comes to the company for the first day after he returns to China from abroad. How do the Chinese pass the time of day with one another? Now here comes Li Lin with a handful of newpaper and letters. Mike warmly exchanges a greeting with her and extends his hand to her. Promptly Li responds by passing over all the newspapers and letters.

Mǎikē：Hi， Lǐ Lín. Nǐ hǎo!
麦克：Hi，李 琳。你 好！
Mike：Hi，Li Lin!

Lǐ Lín：Ō，Mǎizǒng. Nǐ hǎo! Nǐ hǎo!
李 琳：噢，麦总。 你 好，你 好。
Li Lin：Oh，it's you，Maizong. Good morning!

Mǎikē：Yes.（Extending his hand)
麦克：Yes.

Lǐ Lín：Nǐ hǎo! Nǐ hǎo! How nice to see you back!（newspapers and letters scatter about the floor when she extends her hand to him.)
李 琳：你 好！你 好！ How nice to see you back!
Li Lin：Good morning! How nice to see you back!

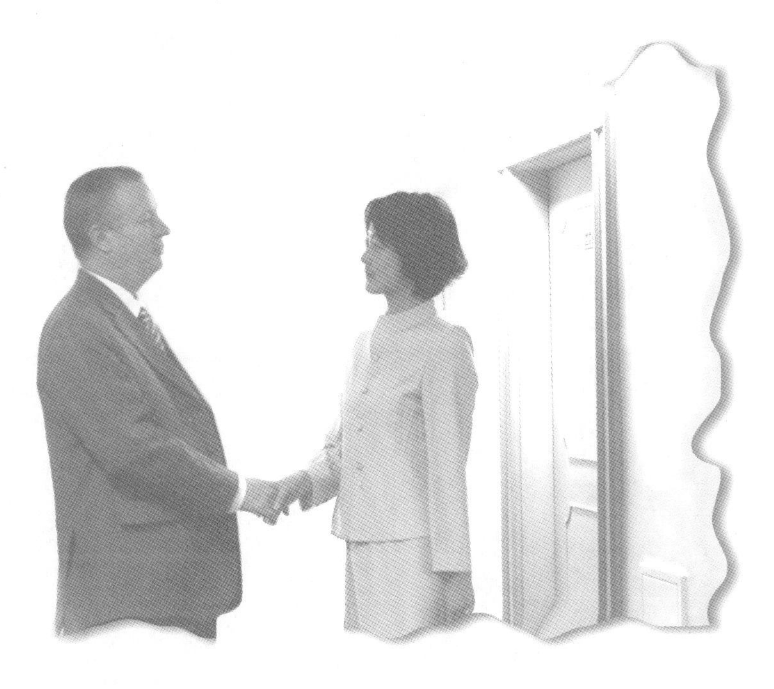

B

Mike exchanges a greeting with the staff in the office upon entering.

Mǎikē：Hello，dàjiā hǎo！
麦克：Hello，大家 好！
Mike：Hello，everybody！

Everybody stands up

Dàjiā：Màizǒng hǎo！
大家：麦总 好！
Everybody：Good morning，Maizong！

Going up to each of the staff members Mike says hello and shakes hands with them.

Mǎikē：Nǐ hǎo！
麦克：你 好！
Mike：Good morning！

A：Màizǒng hǎo！
A：麦总 好！
A：Good morning，Maizong！

Mǎikē：Nǐ hǎo！
麦克：你 好！
Mike：Good morning！

B：Nǐ hǎo！
B：你 好！
B：Good morning！

C is pouring water into his mug and greets Mike from behind. Mike turns round, but realizes C is now on his right side. Thus the formula involves his turning around.

C：Màizǒng hǎo!
C：麦总　好!
C：Good morning, Maizong!

Màikè：Nǐ hǎo!
麦克：你 好!
Mike：Good morning!

Accidentally Mike knocks down an electronic toy that begins talking loudly.

Gōngyìpǐn：Nǐ hǎo!
工艺品：你 好!
Toy：Hello!

Màikè：Nǐ hǎo!
麦克：你 好!
Mike：Hello!

Mike turns round but sees no one there before he catches sight of the toy. Everybody shares the fun with a chorus of laughing.

词　语　Word List

1.你	nǐ	(代)	you (singular)	*(pron.)*
2.好	hǎo	(形)	good, nice	*(adj.)*
3.麦克	Màikè	(专名)	Mike	*(pn.)*
4.李琳	Lǐ Lín	(专名)	name of a person	*(pn.)*
5.噢	ō	(叹)	oh	*(int.)*
6.总	zǒng	(名)	general, always	*(n.)*
7.大家	dàjiā	(代)	everyone	*(pron.)*
8.工艺品	gōngyìpǐn	(名)	handicraft article	*(n.)*

语言点链接 Language Points

三声连读变调 The change of the third tones in succession

汉语中两个或两个以上音节连读时，有时会发生语流音变。当两个三声的音节连在一起读时，前面的三声变成二声。如：本课的“Nǐ hǎo”，其实际读音是“Ní hǎo”。

Sound shifts are likely to take place in the speech stream when two or more syllables stand side by side in a string. Thus it follows that two third tones in succession result in a second tone for the foregoing syllable while the third tone of the accompanied syllable remains unchanged. E.g. “Nǐ hǎo” in the text is read as “Ní hǎo!”.

练习 Exercises

一、请听录音或跟着老师读。

Listen to the recording or read after the demonstration.

nī → n ī → nī
ní → n í → ní
nǐ → n ǐ → nǐ
nì → n ì → nì

hāo → h āo → hāo
háo → h áo → háo
hǎo → h ǎo → hǎo
hào → h ào → hào

mái → m ái → mái
mǎi → m ǎi → mǎi
mài → m ài → mài

līn → l īn → līn
lín → l ín → lín
lǐn → l ǐn → lǐn
lìn → l ìn → lìn

kē → k ē → kē
ké → k é → ké
kě → k ě → kě
kè → k è → kè

zōng → z ōng → zōng
zǒng → z ǒng → zǒng
zòng → z òng → zòng

lī → l ī → lī
lí → l í → lí
lǐ → l ǐ → lǐ
lì → l ì → lì

dā → d ā → dā
dá → d á → dá
dǎ → d ǎ → dǎ
dà → d à → dà

jiā → j　iā → jiā
jiá → j　iá → jiá
jiǎ → j　iǎ → jiǎ
jià → j　ià → jià

yī → y　ī → yī
yí → y　í → yí
yǐ → y　ǐ → yǐ
yì → y　ì → yì

gōng → g　ōng → gōng
gǒng → g　ǒng → gǒng
gòng → g　òng → gòng

pīn → p　īn → pīn
pín → p　ín → pín
pǐn → p　ǐn → pǐn
pìn → p　ìn → pìn

二、听录音并熟读下面的句子。

Listen to the recording and read the following sentences till you learn them by heart.

1. Nǐ hǎo! Màikè.
   你 好！麦克。
2. Nǐ hǎo! Lǐ Lín.
   你 好！ 李 琳。
3. Màikè, nǐ hǎo!
   麦克， 你 好！
4. Lǐ Lín, nǐ hǎo!
   李 琳，你 好！
5. Màizǒng hǎo!
   麦总　　好！
6. Dàjiā hǎo!
   大家　好！

三、跟读并辨别下面音节

Read the following syllables after the demonstration and try to tell one from the other.

dàjiā—dǎjiǎ
nǐhǎo—nínhǎo
lǐlín—lǐlì
màikē—mǎikōu

四、听读下面音节，注意三声音节连读的读音

Listen to the following syllables with special attention to the tone shift in the successive third tones.

hěnhǎo
jiǎntǎo
nǐhǎo
nǐzǒu
qǐpǎo
lǐxiǎng

五、请让我们一起再学习几个常用的词语，然后做练习。

Learn more useful words before you do the exercises.

补充词语 Supplementary Words

您	nín	(代)	you (a polite form)	*(pron.)*
们	men	(助)	*(suffix for plurality)*	*(aux.)*

选择填空 Fill in the Blanks with Appropriate Words

nǐ hǎo (你好)　　nín hǎo (您好)　　nǐmen hǎo (你们好)

1.A：Nǐ hǎo! Màizǒng.
A：你 好！麦总。
B：______________!

2. A：＿＿＿＿＿＿＿＿！
   B：Nǐ hǎo!
   B：你 好！

3. A：Nǐmen hǎo!
   A：你们　好！
   B、C：＿＿＿＿＿＿＿＿！

4. A：Nín hǎo!
   A：您　好！
   B：＿＿＿＿＿＿＿＿！

5. A：Lǐ Lín hǎo!
   A：李 琳　好！
   B：ō, Màizǒng.
   B：噢，麦总。＿＿＿＿＿＿＿＿！

6. A、B：Nǐ hǎo!
   A、B：你　好！
   C：＿＿＿＿＿＿＿＿！

六、把下面表达相同意思的汉字、拼音、英文用线连起来。

Connect the equivalent expressions written in Chinese characters, *pinyin* and English in the three columns with a line.

1. 你好！ Susan.	a. Nǐ hǎo! Susan.	(1) Hello, everybody!
2. Ailin，你好！	b. Dàjiā hǎo!	(2) Hi, Ailin!
3. 你好！	c. Nǐ hǎo!	(3) How do you do!
4. 大家好！	d. Ailin, nǐ hǎo!	(4) How are you, Susan.

七、下面的情景用汉语你知道该怎么说吗？请试一试。

Try to express yourself in the following situations.

1. 在公司门前遇到你的同事 Benz，请你用汉语跟他打招呼。
   How would you greet your colleague Benz in Chinese when you meet him at the company's entrance?

2. 你去机场接客户，见面时他先对你说"您好"，请你用汉语回答他。
   How would you reply in Chinese when your customer greets you with a "您好" at the airport?

3. 你向一位老人问路，你应该先礼貌地跟他打招呼。请你用汉语说。
   How would you begin asking an old man the way with greetings in Chinese?

4. 麦克要向一位大学生了解产品的市场，他首先要用中文和这位大学生打招呼，你看他用哪种方式打招呼比较合适。
   Mike begins his request for information about the product marketing from a college student with greetings. What do you think are the Chinese expressions appropriate to the occasion?

5. 麦克来到幼儿园接孩子，他先要和幼儿园的老师打招呼，还要和小朋友打招呼，请你帮他用汉语说。
   One day Mike comes to collect his child from the kindergarten. He exchanges greetings with the teachers and says hello to all the kids there. Help him express himself in Chinese.

八、汉字点击。

Open the CD to view the characters.

请通过光盘点击认读、书写下面的汉字。请注意汉字书写时的笔顺。

Read and write the following Chinese characters by double clicking the button, focusing your attention on the stroke-order in writing.

你　好　噢　大　家　麦　总　李　琳

自我评估 Self-assessment

1. 你用了多长时间学会本课的问候语？
   How long does it take you to learn the Chinese greetings covered in the text?

2.你认为学汉语有意思吗?

Do you think Chinese is interesting to learn?

3.你有信心学好汉语吗?

Are you confident that you will learn Chinese well?

文化点击 Cultural Points

“你”和“您”的区别

The difference between “nǐ” and “nín”

“你”和“您”都是第二人称单数的面称用语。“你”是一般的称谓，用在同辈或比自己辈分小的人身上，还可以用在较熟悉的朋友之间的互称；“您”是用在对长辈或上级的面称，表示尊敬。

Both nǐ and nín are pronouns of“you”. The former is generally used with colleagues of one's age, younger people, close friends or acquaintances. The latter is applied to elders or higher-ranking officers as a respectful form of addressing.

Dì-sān kè　Xièxie nǐ
第 3 课　谢谢 你
Lesson 3　Thank You

导学 Guiding Remarks

你知道中国人在什么情况下需要表示感谢吗？请看下面的情景，你会了解一些用法的。在合适的时候你能用上，那样中国人会对你更友好的。

When do the Chinese people say "thank you"? You will understand the expressions better after you learn the following situational dialogues. Try to use them on occasions appropriate to the subject, and you will win friendship from more Chinese people.

A

A waiter opens the door for him when Mike comes to the entrance.

Mǎikè：Xièxie!
麦克：谢谢!
Mike：Thank you !

Fúwùyuán：Bú kèqi.
服务员：不客气。
Keeper：You're welcome.

Li Lin brings Mike a cup of tea.

Mǎikè：Xièxie!
麦克：谢谢!
Mike：Thank you!

Lǐ Lín：Bú kèqi.
李 琳：不 客气。
Li Lin：My pleasure.

When Mike takes out his cell phone from his bag, a piece of paper drops out. Li Lin picks it up for him.

Màikè：Xièxie!
麦克：谢谢!
Mike：Thank you!

Lǐ Lín：Bú yòng xiè.
李 琳：不 用 谢。
Li Lin：Don't mention it.

Voice from the other end

The other end：What?

麦克：I am sorry. I was talking to my colleague here.

B

Mike starts his computer. In spite of all his efforts it does not work.

Màikè：Lǐ Lín, bāng yí gè máng.
麦克：李琳， 帮 一个 忙。
Mike：Li Lin, lend me a hand, will you?

Li Lin comes over, checks the system and connections, and finally spots the disconnected plug. She plugs it in the wall socket. and wins an instant success.

Màikè: A! Xièxie nǐ! Xièxie nǐ!
麦克：啊！谢谢 你！谢谢 你！
Mike: Ah, Thank you! And thank you again!

Lǐ Lín: Bú kèqi.
李 琳：不 客气。
Li Lin: Not at all.

词 语 Word List

1.谢谢	xièxie	(动)	to thank, thanks	*(v.)*
2.服务员	fúwùyuán	(名)	waiter, person at sb's service	*(n.)*
3.不	bú	(副)	not	*(adv.)*
4.客气	kèqi	(形)	polite	*(adj.)*
5.用	yòng	(动)	need, to use	*(v.)*
6.帮	bāng	(动)	to help	*(v.)*
7.一	yī	(数)	a, one	*(num.)*
8.个	gè	(量)	*(a measure word)*	*(mw.)*
9.忙	máng	(名)	help	*(n.)*
10.啊	a	(叹)	ah	*(int.)*

语言点链接 Language Points

"不"和"一"的变调

Tone shifts for "bù" and "yī"

汉语中"不"的本来声调是"bù",当"不"在四声音节前时读二声，如：课文中"bú kèqi"；当"不"在其余声调的音节前面或单说时发本调四声，如："bù lái"。

"一"的本调是"yī"，当"一"单说时，读本调一声，即读为"yī"；当"一"在一、二、三声音节前时，读四声，如"yìbān、yìmáo、yìbǎi"；当"一"在四声音节前时，读二声，如"yíduàn"。

Chinese "bù" is originally in the fourth tone, but it shifts to the second tone when followed by a syllable in the fourth tone, as in "bú kèqi", and remains unchanged when it stands alone or is followed by a syllable in other tones, as in "bù lái".

"yī" is generally pronounced in the first tone when standing by itself, but the tone shifts to the fourth when followed by syllables in the first, second or third, as in "yìbān、yì máo、yìbǎi". It also shifts to the second tone when preceding a fourth-tone syllable, as in "yíduàn".

练习 Exercises

一、请听录音或跟着老师读。

Listen to the recording or read after the teacher.

xiē → x iē → xiē
xié → x ié → xié
xiě → x iě → xiě
xiè → x iè → xiè

bū → b ū → bū
bú → b ú → bú
bǔ → b ǔ → bǔ
bù → b ù → bù

kē → k ē → kē
ké → k é → ké
kě → k ě → kě
kè → k è → kè

qī → q ī → qī
qí → q í → qí
qǐ → q ǐ → qǐ
qì → q ì → qì

yōng → y ōng → yōng
yóng → y óng → yóng
yǒng → y ǒng → yǒng
yòng → y òng → yòng

fū → f ū → fū
fú → f ú → fú
fǔ → f ǔ → fǔ
fù → f ù → fù

wū → w ū → wū
wú → w ú → wú
wǔ → w ǔ → wǔ
wù → w ù → wù

yuān → y uān → yuān
yuán → y uán → yuán
yuǎn → y uǎn → yuǎn
yuàn → y uàn → yuàn

bāng → b　āng → bāng
bǎng → b　ǎng → bǎng
bàng → b　àng → bàng

māng → m　āng → māng
máng → m　áng → máng
mǎng → m　ǎng → mǎng

gē → g　ē → gē
gé → g　é → gé
gě → g　ě → gě
gè → g　è → gè

二、听录音并熟读下面的句子。

Listen to the recording and read the following sentences till you learn them by heart.

1. Xièxie.
谢谢!

2. Xièxie nǐ!
谢谢 你!

3. Bú kèqi.
不 客气。

4. Bú yòng xiè.
不 用 谢。

5. Bāng yí gè máng.
帮 一 个 忙。

三、跟读并辨别下面音节。

Read the following sentences till you are able to tell one from the other.

xièxie–xiěxie
kèqi–héqi
búyòng–hùnòng
fúwù–húlu

四、读下面音节，注意“不”和“一”的发音。

Read the following syllables, paying attention to the tone shifts in bū and yī.

bù gān	yì chē
bù jiā	yì tiān
bù lái	yì bān
bù néng	yì nián
bù zǒu	yì pān
bù hǎo	yì qǐ
bú qù	yì miǎo
bú kàn	yí gè
bú shì	yí dìng

五、请让我们一起再学习几个常用的词语，然后做练习。

Learn more useful words before you do the exercises.

补充词语 Supplementary Words

多	duō	(形)	many, more	*(adj.)*
非常	fēicháng	(副)	extremely	*(adv.)*
感谢	gǎnxiè	(动)	to thank	*(v.)*

选择填空 Fill in the Blanks with Appropriate Words

bú kèqi(不客气)　　bú yòng xiè(不用谢)

xièxie nǐ(谢谢你)　　xièxie nǐmen(谢谢你们)

1. A：Màizǒng，fēicháng gǎnxiè！

   A：麦总，　非常　感谢！

   B：________________________。

2. A：________________________！

   B：Bú yòng xiè.

   B：不　用　谢。

3. A: Duō xiè! Duō xiè!
A: 多 谢! 多 谢!
B: ______________________!

4. A: Xièxie nǐmen!
A: 谢谢 你们!
B: ________________!

5. A: Xièxie nǐ!
A: 谢谢 你!
B: ______________________!

6. A: Lǐ Lín
A: 李琳, ____________!
B: Bú yòng xiè.
B: 不 用 谢。

7. A: Màizǒng, Lǐ Lín
A: 麦总, 李 琳, ________!
B: Bú kèqi.
B: 不 客气。

8. A: Fēicháng gǎnxiè!
A: 非常 感谢!
B: ________________!

六、把下面表达相同意思的汉字、拼音、英文用线连起来。

Connect the equivalent expressions in *pinyin*, characters and English in the three columns with a line.

1. 谢谢你!	a. Fēicháng gǎnxiè!	(1) Not at all.
2. 不客气。	b. Bú yòng xiè.	(2) Thank you very much.
3. 非常感谢!	c. Bú kèqi.	(3) Don't mention it.
4. 不用谢。	d. Xièxie nǐ!	(4) Thank you!

七、下面的情景用汉语你知道该怎么说吗？请试一试。

Try to express yourself in the following situations.

1.你的钱包掉在地上，别人帮你拣起来交给了你，请你用汉语说出对他表示感谢的话。

How do you express your gratitude in Chinese to a man who returns the wallet you have lost?

2.你向人问路，别人告诉了你，临走你用汉语向他表示感谢。

How do you say "thank you" in Chinese to a person you have asked the way?

3.你帮了别人一个忙，他向你说"谢谢"，请你用汉语表示客气。

How do you reply in Chinese to a man who is saying "thank you" for the help you have given him?

4.你的钥匙找不到了，同事帮你找到了，你用汉语对他表示感谢。

How do you say "thank you" to your colleague who returns the key you have lost?

八、汉字点击。

Open the CD to view the characters.

请通过光盘点击认读、书写下面的汉字。请注意汉字书写时的笔顺。

Open the CD and read the following characters with special attention to their stroke-order in writing.

谢 不 客 气 用 啊 服 务 员 帮 一 个 忙

自我评估 Self-assessment

1.学习这一课你用了多长时间？

How much time have you spent in learning the text?

2.你在生活中能主动用上汉语吗？

Do you have any chance to use Chinese on your own initiative?

3.你喜欢汉字吗？

Do you like Chinese characters?

文化点击 Cultural Points

什么时候说"谢谢"？ When does one say "Thank you"?

传统上，中国人在真正接受别人的帮助时才说感谢的话。比如，你拣到了他丢失的东西还给他，他会对你说"谢谢"；再比如，当你在公共汽车或地铁上给人让个坐位时，他们会对你说"谢谢"。与西方国家不同的是，中国人在很多场合是不说或很少说"谢谢"的。比如，当听到别人的赞扬时，传统的中国人是不说"谢谢"的；在服务行业，一般是消费者对服务员说"谢谢"，服务员很少因为你给他提供了赚钱的机会而对你说"谢谢"；中国的上级对下级也很少说"谢谢"，哪怕是你给他提供了很大的帮助。

Traditionally a Chinese says "thank you" only when a favour has been done for him. His thanks goes, for example, to a person who returns him a lost item, or to someone who offers him a seat on the bus or in the subway. Unlike westerners, Chinese people don't often verbalize their thanks for complimentary remarks. Chinese consumers do thank waiters for their service, but the latter seldom return their thankfulness. Similarly, a Chinese person of higher authority doesn't often acknowledge a favour, however impressive it may be, to his/her junior partner.

Dì-sì kè　Wǒ shì Lǐ Lín
第4课　我是李琳
Lesson 4　My Name Is Li Lin

导学 Guiding Remarks

这一课我们要学自我介绍了。中国人自我介绍的话有很多，我们先来了解一下最简单有用的。学会了这些，你就知道怎么和不认识的中国人搭话了。

This lesson is about self-introduction. There are many Chinese expressions for the purpose. After learning the simple and useful ones, you will be able to start a conversation with those Chinese you only have no acquaintance with.

A

John Smith pays his first visit to the office after his arrival in Beijing.

John：Xiǎojiě, wǒ shì John Smith.
John：小姐，我 是 John Smith。
John：Hi, Miss, my name is John Smith.

Lǐ Lín：Nǐ hǎo! Nǐ hǎo! Smith xiānsheng.
李 琳：你 好！你 好！ Smith 先生。(extending her hand)
Li Lin：How do you do, Mr. Smith.

John：Nǐ hǎo!
John：你 好！(Shaking hands with her.)
John：How do you do!

Lǐ Lín：Wǒ shì zǒngjīnglǐ zhùlǐ Lǐ Lín.
李 琳：我 是 总经理 助理 李 琳。
Li Lin：I am an assistant to the General Manager. My name is Li Lin.

John：Nǐ hǎo! Lǐ Lín.
John：你 好！李 琳。
John：Nice to meet you, Li Lin.

Lǐ Lín：Nǐ hǎo!
李 琳：你 好！
Li Lin：Nice to meet you too.

B

Liu Li, a visitor from the Guangdong cosmetics company, is waiting in the reception room, Here comes Mike.

Màikè：Nǐ hǎo!Nǐ shì
麦克：你 好！你 是——
Mike：Excuse me, but you are...

Liú Lì：Wǒ shì Guǎngdōng gōngsī de Liú Lì.
刘 力：我 是 广东 公司 的 刘 力。(Handshaking)
Liu Li：My name is Liu Li from the Guangdong company.

Màikè：Nǐ hǎo!Wǒ shì Màikè.
麦克：你 好！我 是 麦克。
Mike：Glad to meet you!My name is Michael Black.

Liú Lì：Nǐ hǎo!Màizǒng.
刘 力：你 好！麦总。
Liu Li：Glad to meet you too, Maizong!

词 语 Word List

1.我	wǒ	(代)	I, me	(*pron.*)
2.是	shì	(动)	be, is, are, was, were	(*v.*)
3.小姐	xiǎojiě	(名)	miss	(*n.*)
4.经理	jīnglǐ	(名)	manager	(*n.*)
5.助理	zhùlǐ	(名)	assistant	(*n.*)
6.刘力	Liú Lì	(专名)	name of a person	(*pn.*)
7.广东	Guǎngdōng	(专名)	name of a province	(*pn.*)
8.公司	gōngsī	(名)	company	(*n.*)
9.的	de	(助)	of	(*aux.*)

语言点链接 Language Points

轻声 The light tone

汉语有的词语末尾的音节读音很轻，很短，没有明显的高低变化，叫轻声音节。如本课中的“先生”。轻声音节在书写时不标声调，其实际读音是前面的音节重读，后面的音节轻轻带出即可。

Some Chinese syllables have a light and brief ending without much speech variation known as the light tone, as “xiānsheng” (mister) in this lesson. The light tones are written without a tone mark. Its utterance may be realized by laying a stress on the first syllable and leaving the following syllable unstressed.

练 习 Exercises

一、请听录音或跟着老师读。

Listen to the recording or read after the teacher.

xiāo → x iāo → xiāo　　jiē → j iē → jiē
xiáo → x iáo → xiáo　　jié → j ié → jié
xiǎo → x iǎo → xiǎo　　jiě → j iě → jiě
xiào → x iào → xiào　　jiè → j iè → jiè

wō → w ō → wō
wǒ → w ǒ → wǒ
wò → w ò → wò

gōng → g ōng → gōng
gǒng → g ǒng → gǒng
gòng → g òng → gòng

dē → d ē → dē
dé → d é → dé

zhū → zh ū → zhū
zhú → zh ú → zhú
zhǔ → zh ǔ → zhǔ
zhù → zh ù → zhù

guāng → g uāng → guāng
guǎng → g uǎng → guǎng
guàng → g uàng → guàng

shī → sh ī → shī
shí → sh í → shí
shǐ → sh ǐ → shǐ
shì → sh ì → shì

sī → s ī → sī
sǐ → s ǐ → sǐ
sì → s ì → sì

jīng → j īng → jīng
jǐng → j ǐng → j ǐng
jìng → j ìng → jìng

liū → l iū → liū
liú → l iú → liú
liǔ → l iǔ → liǔ
liù → l iù → liù

dōng → d ōng → dōng
dǒng → d ǒng → dǒng
dòng → d òng → dòng

二、听录音并熟读下面的句子。

Read the following sentences till you learn them by heart.

1. Wǒ shì zǒngjīnglǐ zhùlǐ Lǐ Lín.
   我 是 总经理 助理 李 琳。

2. Wǒ shì John Smith.
   我 是 John Smith。

3. Wǒ shì Guǎngdōng gōngsī de Liú Lì.
   我 是 广东 公司 的 刘 力。

4. Wǒ shì Màikè.
   我 是 麦克。

三、跟读并辨别下面音节。

Read the following syllables till you are able to tell one from the other.

xiǎojiě–xiǎojié
jīnglǐ–jìnglǐ
zhùlǐ–zhǔlì
gōngsī–gōngshì

四、听读下面音节，注意轻声的读音。

Listen to the following syllables. focusing your attention on the light tones.

xièxie	xiǎojie	bāozi
kèqi	zěnme	hǎole
xiānsheng	láiba	péngyou

五、请让我们一起再学习几个常用的词语，然后做练习。

Learn more useful words before you do the excises.

补充词语 Supplementary Words

新	xīn	(形)	new	*(adj.)*
来	lái	(动)	to come	*(v.)*
新来的	xīn lái de		new comer	
欢迎	huānyíng	(动)	to welcome	*(v.)*

选择填空 Fill in the Blanks with Appropriate Words

nǐ hǎo(你好) wǒ shì(我是)
wǒmen shì(我们是) xīn lái de(新来的)

1. A：Nǐ hǎo! Wǒ shì Lǐ Lì.
A：你 好！ 我 是 李 力。
B：__________________!

2. A、B: Màizǒng, nín hǎo! xīn lái de.
A、B: 麦总， 您 好！ ___________ 新 来 的。
C: Nǐmen hǎo!
C: 你们 好！

3. A: Nǐ hǎo! Wǒ shì
A: 你 好！ 我 是___________。
B: Huānyíng nǐ!
B: 欢迎 你！

4. A: Nǐ hǎo! Wǒ shì Lǐ Lín.
A: 你 好！ 我 是 李 琳。
B: Nǐ hǎo! Liú Lì.
B: 你 好！ ___________ 刘 力.

5. A: Nǐ hǎo! Wǒmen shì
A: 你 好， 我们 是___________。
B: Nǐmen hǎo!
B: 你们 好！

6. A: Jīnglǐ, xīn lái de.
A: 经理，___________ 新 来 的。
B: Huānyíng! Huānyíng!
B: 欢迎！ 欢迎！

六、把下面表达相同意思的汉字、拼音、英文用线连起来。

Connect the equivalent sentences in *pinyin*, characters and English in the three columns with a line.

1. 我是小王。	a. Nǐ hǎo.	(1) Hello!
2. 你好！	b. Wǒ shì Xiǎo Wáng.	(2) I am the general manager.
3. 我是总经理。	c. Wǒ shì zǒngjīnglǐ.	(3) My name is Xiao Wang.

七、下面的情景用汉语你知道该怎么说吗？请试一试。

Try to express yourself in the following situations.

1. 你第一次和一位中国人见面，请用汉语介绍自己。

   Introduce yourself in Chinese when you meet a Chinese person for the first time.

2. 你想向中国人推销自己的产品，请你先介绍自己。

   Introduce yourself to the Chinese businessmen before your sales promotion.

3. 现在你给不熟悉的人打电话，请你用汉语告诉对方你是谁。

   Begin your telephone conversation by a self-introduction in Chinese with some one you don't know.

4. 你来到一个新单位做经理，同事们都不认识你，先用汉语自己介绍一下吧。

   Introduce yourself as a newly appointed manager to your staff members.

八、汉字点击。

Open the CD to view the characters.

请通过光盘点击认读、书写下面的汉字。请注意汉字书写时的笔顺。

Open the CD and read the following characters with special attention to the stroke-order in writing.

小　姐　我　是　公　司　经　理　的　助　理　刘　力

自我评估 Self-assessment

1. 现在你会和不认识的人搭话了吗？

   Do you know how to start a conversation with people you wish to make an acquaintance with?

2. 你会说多少汉语了？

   What progress have you made in spoken Chinese?

3.试着去和中国人聊天，看他们能听懂你说的话吗。

Try to talk with the local Chinese and see if they understand you.

文化点击 Cultural Points

中国人的姓名 Chinese Names

中国人的名字有两部分，前面是姓，后面是名。如："王大可"，他的姓是"王"，名是"大可"。大多数姓是一个字，叫单姓，少数是两个字，叫复姓，如"欧阳、司马"等。名一般是一个字或两个字，极少数是两个字以上。

A Chinese name consists of two parts: the surname precedes the given name. In Wáng Dàkě, for example, Wáng is his surname whereas Dàkě the given name. One-character surnames account for a great percentage of the total. Only a small number of surnames are formed by two characters, such as Ōuyáng or Sīmǎ. There is a common choice between one character and two for one's given name with the exception of a few such names containing three or more characters.

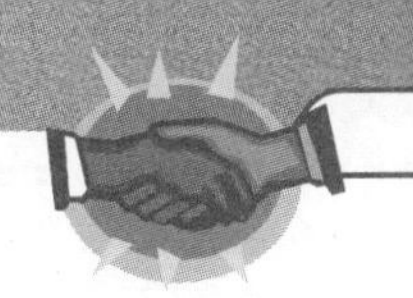

Dì-wǔ kè Huānyíng
第 5 课 欢迎
Lesson 5 Welcome

导学 Guiding Remarks

如果你到中国人的家中或工作单位去，好客的中国人会对你表示他们真诚的欢迎的。学会了这几句表示欢迎的话，在有人来访时，你就知道说什么了。

You will be cordially greeted at a Chinese home or in a company by the hospitable host. Try to learn some useful expressions and use them with your visitors.

课文 Text

A

John comes to the General Manager's office.

John：Nǐ hǎo，Màikē！
John：你 好， 麦克！
John：Hello，Mike!

Màikē：Nǐ hǎo！Nǐ hǎo！Huānyíng！Huānyíng！
麦克：John，my friend. 你 好！你 好！ 欢迎！ 欢迎！
Mike：Hello，John，my friend. Welcome！

Handshaking and patting each other on the shoulder.

John：Jiàndào nǐ hěn gāoxìng.
John：见到 你 很 高 兴。
John：Glad to see you here.

Màikē：Zài Běijīng jiàndào nǐ wǒ yě hěn gāoxìng.
麦克：在 北京 见到 你 我 也 很 高兴。
Mike：Glad to see you in Beijing！

B

BM China Branch is to hold a reception in honour of the VIP customers to celebrate the 10th anniversary of its founding. At the front gate Wang Guang is greeting the guests one after another.

Wāng Guāng：Nǐ hǎo! Huānyíng! Huānyíng!
王 光：你 好！ 欢 迎！ 欢迎！
Wang Guang：Good morning! Welcome to BM!

Liú Lì：Nǐ hǎo!
刘 力：你 好！
Liu Li：Good morning!

Li Lin comes over and shakes hands with Liu Li.

Lǐ Lín：Nǐ hǎo! Liú Lì，huānyíng nǐ!
李 琳：你 好！刘 力， 欢迎 你！
Li Lin：How nice to see you, Liu Li. Welcome!

Liú Lì：Nǐ hǎo! Lǐ Lín.
刘 力：你 好！李 琳。
Liu Li：How are you, Li Lin?

Liu Li presses her hand firmly. Seeing her frowning he lets go.

词 语 Word List

1.见	jiàn	(动)	to see	*(v.)*
2.到	dào	(动)	to arrive, also used as a complement	*(v.)*
3.很	hěn	(副)	very	*(adv.)*
4.高兴	gāoxìng	(形)	glad	*(adj.)*
5.在	zài	(介)	at, in, on	*(prep.)*
6.北京	Běijīng	(专名)	Beijing	*(pn.)*
7.也	yě	(副)	also, too	*(adv.)*
8.王光	Wáng Guāng	(专名)	name of a person	*(pn.)*

语言点链接 Language Points

"也"的用法 The use of "yě"

"也"是副词，放在动词的前面做状语。汉语的副词一般都是放在动词的前面，而不是像英语那样可以放在动词的后面。例如"我也很好"、"我们都是服务员"，"也"和"都"都是副词，只能放在动词前面做状语。

The adverb yě functions as an adverbial modifier before the verb. Unlike their English equivalents, Chinese adverbs are always placed before a verb. E.g."wǒ yě hěn hǎo", "wǒ men dōu shì fúwùyuán", As an adverbial modifier both yě and dōu are followed by a verb.

练　习　Exercises

一、请听录音或跟着老师读。

Listen to the recording and read after the teacher.

huān → h　uān → huān
huán → h　uán → huán
huǎn → h　uǎn → huǎn
huàn → h　uàn → huàn

jiān → j　iān → jiān
jiǎn → j　iǎn → jiǎn
jiàn → j　iàn → jiàn

hén → h　én → hén
hěn → h　ěn → hěn
hèn → h　èn → hèn

xīng → x　īng → xīng
xíng → x　íng → xíng
xǐng → x　ǐng → xǐng
xìng → x　ìng → xìng

bēi → b　ēi → bēi
běi → b　ěi → běi
bèi → b　èi → bèi

yē → y　ē → yē
yé → y　é → yé
yě → y　ě → yě
yè → y　è → yè

guāng → g　uāng → guāng
guǎng → g　uǎng → guǎng
guàng → g　uàng → guàng

yīng → y　īng → yīng
yíng → y　íng → yíng
yǐng → y　ǐng → yǐng
yìng → y　ìng → yìng

dāo → d　āo → dāo
dáo → d　áo → dáo
dǎo → d　ǎo → dǎo
dào → d　ào → dào

gāo → g　āo → gāo
gǎo → g　ǎo → gǎo
gào → g　ào → gào

zāi → z　āi → zāi
zǎi → z　ǎi → zǎi
zài → z　ài → zài

jīng → j　īng → jīng
jǐng → j　ǐng → jǐng
jìng → j　ìng → jìng

wāng → w　āng → wāng
wáng → w　áng → wáng
wǎng → w　ǎng → wǎng
wàng → w　àng → wàng

二、听录音并熟读下面的句子。

Listen to the recording and read the following sentences till you learn them by heart.

1. Huānyíng! Huānyíng!
   欢迎!　欢迎!

2. Jiàndào nǐ hěn gāoxìng.
   见到 你 很 高兴。

3. Zài Běijīng jiàndào nǐ wǒ yě hěn gāoxìng.
   在 北京 见到 你 我 也 很 高兴。

4. Huānyíng nǐ!
   欢迎 你!

三、跟读并辨别下面音节。

Read the following syllables and try to tell one from the other.

huānyíng—huànrén
gāoxìng—gāoxīn
jiàndào—jiàodǎo
běijīng—bèijǐng

四、把"yě(也)"填在下面句子中合适的地方。

Apply yě to an appropriate place in the following sentences.

1. Nǐ shì zǒngjīnglǐ, wǒ shì zǒngjīnglǐ.
   (　)你(　)是(　)总经理,(　)我(　)是(　)总经理(　)。

2. Lǐ Lín gāoxìng, Liú Lì gāoxìng.
   (　)李琳(　)高兴(　),(　)刘力(　)高兴(　)。

3.　Màikè　zài　Běijīng,　John　zài
(　)麦克(　)在(　)北京(　),(　)John(　)在
Běijīng.
(　)北京(　)。

五、请让我们一起再学习几个常用的词语，然后做练习。

Learn more useful words before you do the exercises.

补充词语 Supplementary Words

光临	guānglín	(动)	presence (of a guest, etc.)	(*v.*)
惠顾	huìgù	(动)	patronize	(*v.*)
客户	kèhù	(名)	client, customer, user	(*n.*)

选择填空 Fill in the Blanks with Appropriate Words

huānyíng nǐ(欢迎你)　　huānyíng nǐmen(欢迎你们)

huānyíng(欢迎)　　huānyíng guānglín(欢迎光临)

1. A: Nǐ hǎo! Wǒ shì jīnglǐ zhùlǐ.
   A:你　好!　我　是　经理　助理。
   B:______________________!

2. A、B: Nǐ hǎo! Wǒmen shì xīn lái de.
   A、B:你　好!　我们　是　新　来　的。
   C:______________________!

3. A: Nǐ hǎo!
   A:你　好!__________________。
   B: Nǐ hǎo!
   B:你　好!

4. A: Nǐ hǎo! Wǒ shì Lǐ Lín.
   A:你　好!　我　是　李　琳。
   B: Nǐ hǎo!
   B:你　好!　________________!

5. A: Wǒ shì nǐmen de kèhù.
A: 我 是 你们 的 客户。
B: Nǐ hǎo! __________ huìgù.
B: 你 好! __________ 惠顾!

6. A: Jīnglǐ, wǒmen shì xīn lái de.
B: 经理, 我们 是 新 来 的!
B: __________!

六、把下面表达相同意思的汉字、拼音、英文用线连起来。

Connect the equivalent sentences in *pinyin*, characters and English in the three columns with a line.

1. 欢迎你们!	a. Jiàndào nǐ hěn gāoxìng.	(1) Glad to see you!
2. 见到你很高兴。	b. Huānyíng nǐmen!	(2) Your presence is appreciated.
3. 欢迎光临!	c. Huānyíng guānglín!	(3) Welcome, all of you!

七、下面的情景用汉语你知道该怎么说吗?请试一试。

Try to express yourself in the following situations.

1. 有中国朋友到你的家中去,请你用汉语对他表示欢迎。
How will you greet a Chinese visitor at home?

2. 你的客户来到你的公司,请你用汉语向他表示欢迎。
Extend a friendly welcome in Chinese to your customer who is visiting your company.

3. 你的朋友在电话中对你说他希望到你的家中做客,你用汉语对他表示欢迎。
Extend an invitation in Chinese to your friend whose wish to visit your place is expressed over the phone.

4.你的公司来了新同事，你要用汉语对他说什么？

How will you greet a colleague who newly joins your company?

八、汉字点击。

Open the CD to view characters.

请通过光盘点击认读、书写下面的汉字。请注意汉字书写时的笔顺。

Open the CD, read and write the following characters, paying attention to their stroke-order.

欢 迎 见 到 很 高 兴 在 北 京 也 王 光

自我评估 Self-assessment

1.学习这课你用了多长时间？

How much time have you spent in learning this text?

2.你认为汉语有意思吗？

Do you think Chinese is interesting?

3.你是否很愿意和中国人用汉语聊天？

Would you like to chat with the Chinese people?

文化点击 Cultural Points

关于握手 Handshaking

中国人在见面时也有握手的习惯。朋友之间、熟人之间、同事之间，在久别重逢时会握手，人们在初次相识时一般也要握手。当然，男女之间的握手时间是不会太长的。但是男女之间握手时，无所谓谁先主动伸出手，很多时候是男的主动握手。

Customarily Chinese friends, colleagues and acquaintances shake hands with one another when they first meet or reunite after long years of separation. Handshaking between men and women may be symbolically brief, but the initiative can be taken by either side although male eagerness often prevails.

Dì-liù kè　Qǐng zuò
第 6 课　请 坐
Lesson 6　Sit Down, Please

导学 Guiding Remarks

当你到单位和中国人见面或到中国人家中做客时，他们会礼貌热情地接待你。请记住本课这几句话，这对你在中国的生活会非常有用的。

When you visit a Chinese company or a family, you often receive a polite warm welcome. Remember all the sentences provided in this text, and you will find them useful in your daily life in China.

A

Li Lin and Wang Guang are greeting guests at the entrance to the dining room.

Wāmg Guāng：Qǐng jìn! Qǐng jìn!
王　光：请　进！请　进！
Wang Guang：Come in, please!

Lǐ Lín：Nǐ hǎo! Qǐng jìn!
李　琳：你　好！　请　进！
Li Lin：Good evening, come in, please!

To everybody

Dàjiā hǎo! Dàjiā qǐng zuò! Qǐng zuò!
大家　好！　大家　请　坐！请　坐！
Good evening, ladies and gentlemen, sit down, please!

B

Mike and John are in the office.

Māikē：Qǐng zuò! Qǐng zuò!
麦克： 请 坐！ 请 坐！
Mike：Take a seat, please!

Li Lin is knocking at the door.

Māikē：Qǐng jìn!
麦克： 请 进！
Mike：Come in, please!

Li Lin pushes the door open and then pours a cup of tea for John.

Lǐ Lín：Qǐng hē chá.
李 琳：请 喝 茶。
Li Lin：Have a cup of tea, please.

John：Xièxie!
John：谢谢！(The tea is so hot that he burns his mouth when he begins to drink. Awkwardly he spills it over.) Oh, My God!
John：Thank you!

Li gives him a piece of tissue paper.

Lǐ Lín：Qǐng yòng zhèige.
李 琳：请 用 这个。
Li Lin：Please use the paper.

John：Xièxie!
John：谢谢！
John：Thanks!

词　语　Word List

1.请	qǐng	(动)	please, to invite, to ask	*(v.)*
2.坐	zuò	(动)	to sit	*(v.)*
3.进	jìn	(动)	to come in	*(v.)*
5.喝	hē	(动)	to drink	*(v.)*
6.茶	chá	(名)	tea	*(n.)*
7.这	zhè	(代)	this	*(pron.)*
8.这个	zhèige		this	

语言点链接　Language Points

"这"的读音　The pronunciations of "zhè"

"这"的本音是zhè，在和数量词语搭配时可以读zhèi的音，也可以读zhè的音。本课中"这个"是"这一个"的简缩形式。汉语中"这一个"、"那（nà，that）一个"中的"一"常常省略，简缩为"这个"、"那个"。

"zhè" is pronounced as "zhè". When followed by a numeral and measure word group, it is pronounced as "zhèi" or "zhè". "zhèige" used in the text is the abbreviated form of "zhè yí gè". "yī" in "zhè yí gè" and "nà yí gè" can be omitted. Hence "zhè yí gè" and "nà yí gè" can be shortened as "zhèige" and "nèige".

练　习　Exercises

一、请听录音或跟着老师读。

Listen to the recording or read after the teacher.

qīng → q īng → qīng	zuō → z uō → zuō
qíng → q íng → qíng	zuó → z uó → zuó
qǐng → q ǐng → qǐng	zuǒ → z uǒ → zuǒ
qìng → q ìng → qìng	zuò → z uò → zuò

jīn → j īn → jīn
jǐn → j ǐn → jǐn
jìn → j ìn → jìn

hē → h ē → hē
hé → h é → hé
hè → h è → hè

chā → ch ā → chā
chá → ch á → chá
chǎ → ch ǎ → chǎ
chà → ch à → chà

二、听录音并熟读下面的句子。

Listen to the recording and read the following sentences till you learn them by heart.

1. Qǐng jìn!
   请 进!

2. Dàjiā qǐng zuò!
   大家 请 坐!

3. Qǐng zuò zhèr.
   请 坐 这儿。

4. Qǐng hē chá.
   请 喝 茶。

5. Qǐng yòng zhèige.
   请 用 这个。

三、跟读并辨别下面音节。

Read the following syllables and try to tell one from the other.

qǐngzuò—qǐluò
hēchá—hēshá
zhèige—shèkē
zuòzhèr—shuōshìr

四、请正确地指出下面音节的声调标注位置，自己试着标一标。

Point out the right position in each syllable for the tone mark to place on. Try to mark them by yourself.

ni	hao	huan	ying	li	lin	man	ye
zhou	gui	jing	huan	bei	lai	hen	guang

五、请让我们一起再学习几个常用的词语，然后做练习。

Learn more commonly used words before you do the exercises.

补充词语　Supplementary Words

吃	chī	(动)	to eat, to take	(*v.*)
糖	táng	(名)	sugar, sweets	(*n.*)

选择填空　Fill in the Blanks with Appropriate Words

hē chá(喝茶)　　qǐng zuò(请坐)　　xièxie(谢谢)

1. A：Qǐng zuò!
   A：　请　坐！
   B：__________！

2. A：__________。
   B：Xièxie!
   B：谢谢！

3. A：Qǐng chī táng.
   A：　请　吃　糖。
   B：__________。

4. A：Lǐ Lín, qǐng
   　　李 琳，　请__________。
   B：Xièxie!
   B：谢谢！

5.A：Màikè，qǐng hē chá.

A： 麦克， 请 喝 茶。

B：__________。

6.A：Xiǎo Wáng

A： 小 王，__________。

B：Xièxie!

B：谢谢!

六、把下面表达相同意思的汉字、拼音、英文用线连起来。

Connect the equivalent sentences in *pinyin*, characters and English in the three columns with a line.

A.请进!	1.Dàjiā qǐng zuò!	(1) sit down, everybody!
B.大家请坐!	2.Qǐng hē chá.	(2) Have a cup of tea, please!
C.请喝茶。	3.Qǐng jìn!	(3) Come in, please!

七、下面的情景用汉语你知道该怎么说吗？请试一试。

Try to express yourself in the following situations.

1.朋友到你家中来做客，你用汉语对他说什么？

One day your friend comes to your place as a guest. How would you greet him in Chinese?

2.你的客户来到你的公司，请你用汉语接待他。

How would you greet your customer in Chinese when he is visiting your company?

3.有人敲门，请你用汉语对他说让他进来的话。

What's the Chinese for "come in, please"? ---phrases that you need when you hear someone knocking at the door.

4.有人要购买你的商品，他正在看，这时你会用汉语对他说什么？

What would you say in Chinese to a customer who is examining your products before he makes his purchases?

八、汉字点击。

Open the CD to view the characters.

请通过光盘点击认读、书写下面的汉字。请注意汉字书写时的笔顺。

Open the CD, read and write the following characters with special attention to the stroke-order.

请 坐 进 喝 茶 个 这

自我评估 Self-assessment

1.学习了这一课，你知道中国人怎样招待客人了吧？

What have you learned about the reception of guests in China from this text?

2.现在如果有位客人到你家中做客，你打算对他说什么？

What would you say in Chinese to a visitor in your place?

3.你还能想出什么接待客户时说的话？

Are there any more Chinese expressions that are applicable to the reception of customers?

文化点击 Cultural Points

中国人待客的礼俗 The Chinese etiquette for the reception of guests

如果你到中国人的家中去，你会发现，他们是非常热情的。他们会请你喝茶、吃糖果、吃水果，有时还会请你吃一些小点心。这时你尽可无拘无束地享用，因为他们是真诚的。可能你已经觉得很丰盛了，但他们还会说："没什么招待你。"或者说："请随便吃一点。"这时你千万不要以为东西真的很少或不好，这只是他们谦虚。当你告别时，好客的主人会邀请你以后再来玩，你也不必认真地去确定时间，因为这是他们的礼貌。

You will receive a warm welcome during your visit to a Chinese family. You are likely to be treated to tea, sweets, fruits or refreshments. Just feel free to enjoy everything, for the sincerity and hospitality of the host should make you feel at home. Perhaps you think the entertainment is rich, but the host would insist that they don't have much to serve, that you just have a taste of whatever you like. This modest attitude should not be taken that their reception of the guests is below par. Before departure, inviting you to come again is often expressed as a friendly gesture for which the arrangement of a date may not be seriously made.

Dì-qī kè Zhè wèi shì Xiǎo Bái
第7课 这位是小白
Lesson 7 This Is Xiao Bai

导学 Guiding Remarks

在中国你一定会遇到介绍不认识的人之间互相认识的情况，这一课就教给你怎样作介绍。

How often have you introduced or been introduced to people since you came to China? The present text will help you learn useful Chinese expressions of introduction.

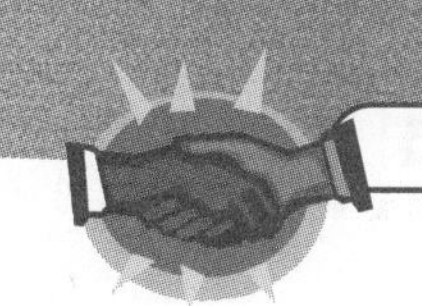

A

The Marketing Manager Wang Guang knocks at the door before he enters Mike's office. Mike introduces him to John. Please take careful note of how these Chinese expressions are used.

Màikē: Zhè wèi shì xiāoshòu bù jīnglǐ Wáng Guāng.
麦克：(to John) 这 位 是 销售 部 经理 王 光。
Zhè wèi shì John Smith.
(to Wáng) 这 位 是 John Smith。
Mike: This is our Sales Manager Wang Guang, and this is John Smith.

Wáng Guāng: Nǐ hǎo!
王 光：你 好！
Wang Guang: How do you do!

John: Nǐ hǎo! Wáng jīnglǐ.
John: 你 好！ 王 经理。
John: How do you do, Manager!

Xiao Bai comes in for John's signature on the prepared document. John introduces them to one another.

Xiǎo Bái: Màizǒng, qǐng nín qiān zì.
小 白：麦总， 请 您 签字。
Xiao Bai: Maizong, will you please sign this document?

Màikē: Zhè wèi shì bàngōngshì mìshū Xiǎo Bái.
麦克：(Signing and talking with John) 这 位 是 办公室 秘书 小 白。
Zhè wèi shì John Smith.
这 位 是 John Smith。
Mike: This is our office secretary Xiao Bai, and this is John Smith.

Xiǎo Bái: Nín hǎo!
小 白：您 好！
Xiao Bai: How do you do!

John：Nǐ hǎo!
John：你 好!
John：How do you do!

B

After Mike and John enter the dining room, Li Lin makes introductions all round.

Lǐ Lín：Zhè wèi shì Màikè, gōngsī de zǒngjīnglǐ. Zhè wèi shì
李 琳：这 位 是 麦克， 公司 的 总经理。 这 位 是……
Li Lin：This is Mike, the General Manager of the company, and this is...

Màikè：Liú Lì xiānsheng. Wǒmen rènshi.
麦克：刘 力 先生。(To Li Lin) 我们 认识。
Mike：Mr. Liu Li. We have met before.

Liú Lì：Nín hǎo!
刘 力：您 好!
Liu Li：Hello!

Màikè：Nǐ hǎo!
麦克：你 好!
Mike：Hello!

They shake hands with one another.

Li Lin introduces John to Liu Li.

Lǐ Lín: Zhè wèi shì John Smith xiānsheng. Zhè wèi shì Liú Lì xiānsheng.
李 琳: 这 位 是 John Smith 先生。 这 位 是 刘 力 先生。
Li Lin: This is John Smith, and this is Mr. Liu Li.

John: Nǐ hǎo, Liú xiānsheng.
John: 你 好, 刘 先生。
John: How do you do, Mr. Liu.

Liú Lì: Nín hǎo, Smith xiānsheng.
刘 力: 您 好, Smith 先生。(Handshaking)
Li Lin: How do you do, Mr. Smith.

词 语 Word List

1. 位	wèi	(量)	(a measure word)	*(mw.)*
2. 小	xiǎo	(形)	young, little	*(adj.)*
3. 小白	Xiǎo Bái	(专名)	(surname of a person)	*(pn.)*
4. 销售	xiāoshòu	(动)	to sell	*(v.)*
5. 部	bù	(名)	section, department	*(n.)*
6. 签字	qiān zì	(名)	to sign, signature	*(n.)*
7. 办公室	bàngōngshì	(名)	office	*(n.)*
8. 秘书	mìshū	(名)	secretary	*(n.)*
9. 我们	wǒmen	(代)	we	*(pron.)*
10. 认识	rènshi	(动)	to know	*(v.)*

语言点链接 Language Points

关于介绍 Introducing People

汉语中把某人介绍给别人时，用的是“这位是”或“这是”，不能说“他（她）是”。如果你要向别人介绍物品时，就只能用“这是”来表达。比如你要向客户介绍你的产品，你可以说“这是我们的新产品，这是男士用的，这是女士用的……”

The Chinese expressions “zhè wèi shì...” and “zhè shì...” are often used to introduce people to one another, but “tā shì...” is not preferred. “Zhè shì...” can also be used to describe objects to people. To explain your products to the customers, you may say “Zhè shì wǒmen de xīn chǎnpǐn, zhè shì nánshì yòng de, zhè shì nǚshì yòng de……” (These are our new products...These are designed for gentlemen... and those are made for ladies...)

练习 Exercises

一、请听录音或跟着老师读。

Listen to the recording or read after the teacher.

wēi → w ēi → wēi
wéi → w éi → wéi
wěi → w ěi → wěi
wèi → w èi → wèi

shōu → sh ōu → shōu
shóu → sh óu → shóu
shǒu → sh ǒu → shǒu
shòu → sh òu → shòu

bān → b ān → bān
bǎn → b ǎn → bǎn
bàn → b àn → bàn

mī → m ī → mī
mí → m í → mí
mǐ → m ǐ → mǐ
mì → m ì → mì

shū → sh ū → shū
shú → sh ú → shú
shǔ → sh ǔ → shǔ
shù → sh ù → shù

xiāo → x iāo → xiāo
xiáo → x iáo → xiáo
xiǎo → x iǎo → xiǎo
xiào → x iào → xiào

bāi → b āi → bāi
bái → b ái → bái
bǎi → b ǎi → bǎi
bài → b ài → bài

qiān → q iān → qiān
qián → q ián → qián
qiǎn → q iǎn → qiǎn
qiàn → q iàn → qiàn

nín → n ín → nín

zī → z ī → zī
zǐ → z ǐ → zǐ
zì → z ì → zì

二、听录音并熟读下面的句子。

Listen to the recording and read the following sentences till you learn them by heart.

1. Zhè wèi shì xiāoshòu bù jīnglǐ Wáng Guāng.
   这 位 是 销售 部 经理 王 光。

2. Zhè wèi shì John.
   这 位 是 John。

3. Zhè wèi shì bàngōngshì mìshū Xiǎo Bái.
   这 位 是 办公室 秘书 小 白。

4. Zhè wèi shì Màikè xiānsheng, gōngsī de zǒngjīnglǐ.
   这 位 是 麦克 先生， 公司 的 总经理。

5. Zhè wèi shì Liú Lì xiānsheng.
   这 位 是 刘 力 先生。

6. Qǐng nín qiān zì.
   请 您 签 字。

三、跟读并辨别下面音节。

Read the following syllables and try to tell one from the other.

shìchǎng—shíchǎng
mìshū—mùshū
qiānzì—qīnzì
zhè wèi—zuòwèi

四、请让我们一起再学习几个常用的词语，然后做练习。

Learn more useful words before you do the exercises.

补充词语 Supplementary Words

朋友	péngyou	(名)	friend	(*n.*)
同事	tóngshì	(名)	colleague	(*n.*)
老板	lǎobǎn	(名)	boss, manager	(*n.*)
爱人	àiren	(名)	wife or husband	(*n.*)

选择填空 Fill in the Blanks with Appropriate Words

wǒ de(我的)　　péngyou(朋友)　　tóngshì(同事)

nǐ hǎo(你好)　　Zhè wèi(这位)

1. A：Xiǎo Wáng, zhè wèi shì wǒ de péngyou.
   A：小王，这位是我的朋友。
   Zhè wèi shì wǒ de tóngshì.
   这位是我的同事。
   B：__________________!
   C：__________________!

2. A：Zhè wèi shì 　　　lǎobǎn. Zhè wèi shì wǒ de
   A：这位是______老板。这位是我的______。
   B：Nǐ hǎo!
   B：你好!
   C：Nǐ hǎo!
   C：你好!

3. A：Zhè wèi shì wǒ de 　　　　　　shì wǒ de tóngshì.
   A：这位是我的______。______是我的同事。
   B：Nǐ hǎo!
   B：你好!
   C：Nǐ hǎo!
   C：你好!

4. A：Lǐ Lín, zhè shì wǒ àiren. Zhè shì Lǐ Lín.
   A：李琳，这是我爱人。这是李琳。
   B：__________________!
   C：Nǐ hǎo.
   C：你好!

五、请用下面的词语试着介绍一下你的办公室成员。

Introduce your staff members with the following words.

先生　　小姐　　经理　　秘书

六、把下面表达相同意思的汉字、拼音、英文用线连起来。

Connect the equivalent sentences in pinyin, characters and English in the three columns with a line.

A.这位是销售部经理王光。
B.这位是办公室秘书小白。
C.这位是公司的总经理麦克先生。
D.请您签字。

1.Zhè wèi shì bàngōngshì mìshu Xiǎo Bái.
2.Zhè wèi shì xiāoshòu bù jīnglǐ Wáng Guāng.
3.Qǐng nín qiān zì.
4.Zhè wèi shì gōngsī de zǒngjīnglǐ Màikè xiānsheng.

(1) Please sign here.
(2) This is the General Manager Mike.
(3) This is the office secretary Xiao Bai.
(4) This is the Marketing Manager Wang Guang.

七、下面的情景用汉语你知道该怎么说吗？请试一试。

Try to express yourself in the following situations.

1.你邀请了几位朋友一起聚会，请你用汉语为他们作介绍。

Introduce your friends to one another in Chinese at a party that you host.

2.中国朋友来到你的家里，请给你爱人和他互相作介绍。

Introduce your wife to the Chinese friend who calls at your house.

3.你带客户去见你的老板，请你用汉语让他们互相认识。

You take a customer to see the manager and introduce them to one another in Chinese.

八、汉字点击。

Open the CD to view the characters.

请通过光盘点击认读、书写下面的汉字。请注意汉字书写时的笔顺。

Open the CD, read and write the following characters with special attention to their stroke-order.

位 销 售 部 办 室 秘 书 白 您 签 字 认 识

自我评估 Self-assessment

1.学习了这一课，你知道怎样在朋友聚会时为他们互相介绍了吧？
Could you introduce people in Chinese at a party after you have learned this text?

2.你现在能用汉语说多少话了？
What progress have you made in spoken Chinese?

3.你的客户能听懂你说的汉语吗？
Can your customers understand you as a Chinese speaker?

文化点击 Cultural Points

介绍他人的顺序 The proper sequence of an introduction

在中国，一般在较为随意的场合介绍人们互相认识时，不太讲究顺序，不很在意地位和性别的差异；但在正式的场合（如会议、谈判）都先介绍地位高的或年长的人。

Generally speaking, Chinese people are not so particular about the personal order of any introduction on informal occasions. Positions and sexes do not suggest much difference. However, in formal introductions (e.g. at a conference or in negotiations) the precedence is always given according to ranking and seniority.

Dì-bā kè　Hǎo de
第8课　好的
Lesson 8　Yes, I Will

导学 Guiding Remarks

在别人要求你做什么事或征询你的意见时你该说什么呢？汉语有多种表达方式。先学会这几句有用的，可以帮你解决一些大问题。

What would you say to a person who asks you a favour or makes a request for your advice? There are many Chinese expressions under this category, of which we shall first deal with the most useful ones for you to settle problems that may arise.

A

Mike enters the office where Li Lin works. Seeing no one there he raises his voice.

Màikē: Lǐ Lín!
麦克：李 琳！
Mike: Li Lin!

Lǐ Lín: āi!
李 琳：哎！(Coming from behind a filing cabinet)
Li Lin: Here!

Màikē: Fā yí gè chuánzhēn gěi zǒngbù.
麦克：发 一 个 传真 给 总部。
Mike: Send a fax to the Head Office, please!

Lǐ Lín: Hǎode.
李 琳：好的。
Li Lin: Yes, I will.

B

Li Lin is going out to buy stationery.

Wáng Guāng：Lǐ Lín, děng yíxià.
王 光：李 琳， 等 一下。
Wang Guang：Li Lin, would you mind waiting a minute?

Li Lin turns round.

Wáng Guāng：Qǐng bāng wǒ yìn yì hé míngpiàn.
王 光：请 帮 我 印 一 盒 名片。
Wang Guang：Will you have a box of visiting cards printed for me?

Lǐ Lín：Hǎode.
李 琳：好的。
Li Lin：Yes, I will.

词　语 Word List

1.哎	āi	(叹)	here	*(int.)*
2.发	fā	(动)	to send	*(v.)*
3.传真	chuánzhēn	(名)	fax	*(n.)*
4.给	gěi	(动)	to give, for, to	*(v.)*
5.总部	zǒngbù	(名)	head office, general headquarters	*(v.)*
6.等	děng	(动)	to wait	*(v.)*
7.一下	yíxià		for a while	
8.印	yìn	(动)	to print	*(v.)*
9.盒	hé	(量)	box	*(mw.)*
10.名片	míngpiàn	(名)	visiting card	*(n.)*

语言点链接 Language Points

1."的" The use of "de"

"的"在句子中起结构助词的作用，代表一种所属关系，如"广东的刘力"；"的"放在一个词语的后面，表示一种所指，如"这是我的"，其实是后面省略了中心语的所属关系，指"我的东西"；"的"在句子末尾，可以表示一种应答的语气，如"好的、是的"，还可以构成"是……的"格式，表示肯定。

"de" often functions as a structural auxiliary word of possession as in "Guǎngdōng de Liú Lì"(Liu Li from Guangdong). When placed after a pronoun, it forms a possessive phrase with the central word omitted. E.g. "zhè shì wǒ de", meaning "It's mine". When used at the end of a sentence, "的" carries a sense of "O.K." as in "hao de" or "Yes" as in "shì de". The sentence pattern "shì… de" thus indicates one's positive assessment.

2. 数字认读 How to read Chinese numerals

汉语数字只需要记住从一到十这10个就可以认读出其余的。下面是数字的书写和读音表。

So long as you learn Chinese numerals from one to ten by heart, you will be able to read any figures written in characters. The following are ten basic characters and their pronunciation.

汉　字	读　音	英　译
一	yī	one
二	èr	two
三	sān	three
四	sì	four
五	wǔ	five
六	liù	six
七	qī	seven
八	bā	eight
九	jiǔ	nine
十	shí	ten
十六	shíliù	sixteen
二十	èrshí	twenty
三十四	sānshísì	thirty four
一百	yìbǎi	one hundred
一千	yìqiān	one thousand
一万	yíwàn	ten thousand
零	líng	zero

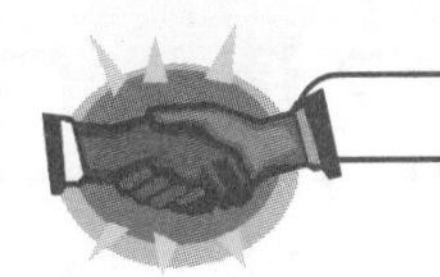

练 习 Exercises

一、请听录音或跟着老师读。

Listen to the recording or read after the teacher.

fā → f ā → fā
fá → f á → fá
fǎ → f ǎ → fǎ
fà → f à → fà

zhēn → zh ēn → zhēn
zhěn → zh ěn → zhěn
zhèn → zh èn → zhèn

dēng → d ēn → dēng
děng → d ěn → děng
dèng → d èn → dèng

yīn → y īn → yīn
yín → y ín → yín
yǐn → y ǐn → yǐn
yìn → y ìn → yìn

míng → m íng → míng
mǐng → m ǐng → mǐng
mìng → m ìng → mìng

chuān → ch uān → chuān
chuán → ch uán → chuán
chuǎn → ch uǎn → chuǎn
chuàn → ch uàn → chuàn

gěi → g ěi → gěi

xiā → x iā → xiā
xiá → x iá → xiá
xià → x ià → xià

hē → h ē → hē
hé → h é → hé
hè → hè → hè

piān → p iān → piān
pián → p ián → pián
piǎn → p iǎn → piǎn
piàn → p iàn → piàn

二、听录音并熟读下面的句子。

Listen to the recording and read the following sentences till you learn them by heart.

1. Fā yí gè chuánzhēn gěi zǒngbù.
发 一 个 传真 给 总部。

2. Qǐng bāng wǒ yìn yì hé míngpiàn.
请 帮 我 印 一 盒 名片。

3. Qǐng děng yíxià.
请 等 一下。

4. Hǎode.
好的。

三、跟读并辨别下面音节。

Read the following syllables and try to tell one from the other.

chuánzhēn–zhuānxīn
zǒngbù–zhǒngzú
míngpiàn–míngtiān
yìhé–yíxià

四、试着读出下面数字。

Read out the following Chinese numerals.

一	二	三	四	五	六	七
八	九	十	四十七	九十八	一百	三万

五、请让我们一起再学习几个常用的词语，然后做练习。

Learn more commonly used words before you do the exercises.

补充词语 Supplementary Words

可以	kěyǐ	(动)	can, be able to	(v.)
买	mǎi	(动)	to buy	(v.)
电脑	diànnǎo	(名)	computer	(n.)

选择填空 Fill in the Blanks with Appropriate Words

kěyǐ(可以)　　hǎode(好的)

1. A: Xiǎo Wáng, kěyǐ bāngwǒ mǎi yí gè diànnǎo ma?
   A: 小　王，　可以　帮　我　买　一　个　电脑　吗？
   B: ________________。

2. A: Qǐng fā yí gè chuánzhēn.
   A: 请　发　一　个　传真。
   B: ________________。

3. A: Wǒ kěyǐ mǎi yí gè diànnǎo ma?
   A: 我　可以　买　一　个　电脑　吗？
   B: ________________。

4. A: Lǐ Lín, qǐng lái yíxià.
   A: 李　琳，　请　来　一下。
   B: ________________。

六、把下面表达相同意思的汉字、拼音、英文用线连起来。

Connect the equivalent sentences in *pinyin*, characters and English in the three columns with a line.

A. 印一盒名片。	1. Yìn yì hé míngpiàn.	(1) O.K.
B. 发一个传真。	2. Děng yíxià.	(2) Send a fax.
C. 等一下。	3. Fā yí gè chuánzhēn.	(3) Get a box of visiting cards printed.
D. 好的。	4. Hǎode.	(4) Wait a minute.

七、下面的情景用汉语你知道该怎么说吗？请试一试。

Try to express yourself in the following situations.

1. 当你的朋友要你帮忙开门时，你用汉语回答他。

   How will you reply in Chinese when your friend asks you to open the door for him?

2. 你用汉语请求别人替你开灯。

What's the Chinese for "turn on the light for me, please!"

3. 你的客户请你介绍一下你的产品，你很痛快地答应他，怎么用汉语说？

How will you recommend your products in Chinese at the request of your customer?

八、汉字点击。

Open the CD to view the characters.

请通过光盘点击认读、书写下面的汉字。请注意汉字书写时的笔顺。

Open the CD, click the buttons, read and write the following characters, paying attention to their stroke-order.

哎　发　传　真　给　部　等　下　印　盒　名　片

自我评估 Self-assessment

1. 你现在知道怎么要求别人为你做什么了吧？

Have you learned the Chinese expressions you need for making a request?

2. 如果你很愿意为别人帮忙，你知道怎么表达了吧？

How will you express yourself in Chinese when you wish to help someone?

3. 你的发音怎么样，中国人能听懂吗？

How is your Chinese pronunciation? Can native Chinese speakers follow you?

文化点击 Cultural Points

称谓　Chinese appellations

中国人的称谓很复杂，同事之间可以称职务，如"麦总、刘经理"等，熟人之间可以直呼其名，或者在姓的前面加上"老、小"来称呼，如"老王、小王"等。比较正式的场合对不熟悉的人一般可以称"先生、女士、太太、小姐"等。

The Chinese system of names and titles is by and large complicated. Titles may be used to address each other among one's colleagues, e.g. "màizǒng" and

"Liú Jīnglǐ". For acquaintances personal names and surnames may be preceded by "lǎo"(old) or "xiǎo"(young). Formal patterns of address include "xiānsheng"(mister, Sir). "nǚshì" (Ms or Mrs), "tàitai"(madam or Mrs) and "xiǎojie"(miss).

Dì-jiǔ kè 第9课 Lesson 9   Duìbuqǐ 对不起 Sorry

导学 Guiding Remarks

你在生活中一定会遇到需要表达歉意的时候，这时可不能不说呀。所以学会道歉是非常必要的。

In our daily life there are faults and failures that one regrets or feels sorry about. An apology, if necessary, is always better than none. Therefore it is advisable for one to learn a few useful apologetic expressions.

A

Xiao Wang was caught in a traffic jam on his way to the office. Now he is in such a hurry that he bumps into someone in the corridor.

Wáng Guāng: Duìbuqǐ!
王　光：(apologizing) 对不起！
Wang Guang: Sorry!

Pushing the door open

Wáng Guāng: Duìbuqǐ! Dǔ chē le.
王　光：对不起！ 堵　车　了。
Wang Guang: Sorry! It was the traffic jam!

Màikè: Zīliào ne?
麦克：资料　呢？
Mike: What about the files?

Wáng Guāng: Ō, zài chē li. Duìbuqǐ!
王　光：噢，在　车　里。对不起！
Wang Guang: Oh, they're left in the car. I am so sorry!

He hurries off to get the files.

B

Wang Guang works with Li Lin's computer. Carelessly he spills water on the table, and knocks over a glass. When Li Lin comes in Wang Guang is busily wiping up the mess with Li's towel.

Wáng Guāng: Duìbuqǐ!
王　光：(Pointing to the broken glass on the ground) 对不起！
Wang Guang: So sorry!

Lǐ Lín: Méi guānxi.
李 琳：没 关系。
Li Lin: Never mind.

Wáng Guāng: Duìbuqǐ!
王 光：(lifting the wet towel)对不起！
Wang Guang: I am sorry!

Lǐ Lín: Méi guānxi.
李 琳：没 关系。
Li Lin: It doesn't matter.

Wáng Guāng: Zhēn duìbuqǐ!
王 光：(Picking up the wet manuscript)真 对不起！
Wang Guang: Terribly sorry!

Lǐ Lín: Á? Méi guānxi.
李 琳：啊？没 关系。(Helplessly)
Li Lin: What? That's O.K.

词　语　Word List

1.对不起	duìbuqǐ		sorry	
2.堵	dǔ	(动)	to jam, to be caught in a traffic jam	(v.)
3.车	chē	(名)	car, bus	(n.)
4.了	le	(助)	used after a verb or verbal phrase to indicate the completion of a real or expected action or a change	(aux.)
5.资料	zīliào	(名)	material	(n.)
6.呢	ne	(语气)	(a interrogative final particle)	(mp.)
7.里	lǐ	(名)	inside, in	(n.)
8.没关系	méi guānxi		never mind, It doesn't matter	
9.真	zhēn	(副)	really, awfully	(adv.)

语言点链接　Language Points

量词（Liàngcí）　Measure words

量词是汉语中一种比较特殊的词类。在表达事物数量时，除了用数词以外，还要在数词后面加上量词。汉语的量词很丰富，不同的事物用不同的量词，同一事物在不同的表达形式下也有不同的量词。表示名词数量的叫名量词，如："一盒、一个"等；表示动作次数的叫动量词，如："一下儿"；表示动作经历时间的叫时量词，如，"一会儿(huìr)"。

Chinese measure words belong to a special part of speech. A numeral and a measure word are used together to indicate the number and quantity under discussion. There are a great deal of measure words in Chinese. As a rule different measure words are applicable to different things or objects. Likewise, the same thing or object preceded by different measure words carries different meanings. There are nominal measure words, e.g. "yì hē", "yí gè", verbal measure words, e.g. "yí xiàr". and time-quantity measure words, e.g. "yí huìr".

下面是本书中出现的部分名词和常用量词的搭配表（数词以“一”为例）：

The collocation of commonly used nouns and measure words (prefixed by “yī”)

名词（拼音） Noun	量词（拼音） Measure word	组合（拼音） Collocation	英译 English
人(rén)	个(gè) / 口 (kǒu)	一个人(yí gè rén)/ 一口人 (yì kǒu rén)	A person A member/a family
书(shū)	本(běn)	一本书(yì běn shū)	A book
笔(bǐ)	枝(zhī)	一枝笔(yì zhī bǐ)	A pen
桌子(zhuōzi)	张(zhāng)	一张桌子(yì zhāng zhuōzi)	A table
椅子(yǐzi)	把(bǎ)	一把椅子(yì bǎ yǐzi)	A chair
电脑(diànnǎo)	台(tái)	一台电脑(yì tái diànnǎo)	A computer
电话(diànhuà)	部(bù)	一部电话(yí bù diànhuà)	A telephone
手机(shǒujī)	部(bù)	一部手机(yí bù shǒujī)	A cell phone
文件(wénjiàn)	份(fèn)	一份文件(yí fèn wénjiàn)	A document
汽车(qìchē)	辆(liàng)	一辆汽车(yí liàng qìchē)	An automobile
传真(chuánzhēn)	份(fèn)	一份传真 (yí fèn chuánzhēn)	A fax
传真机(chuánzhēnjī)	台(tái)	一台传真机 (yì tái chuánzhēnjī)	A fax machine
服务员(fúwùyuán)	位(wèi)/ 个(gè)	一位服务员(yí wèi fúwùyuán)/ 一个服务员(yí gè fúwùyuán)	A waiter
公司(gōngsī)	个(gè)/ 家(jiā)	一个公司(yí gè gōngsī)/ 一家公司(yì jiā gōngsī)	A company
客户(kè hù)	位(wèi)/ 个(gè)	一位客户(yí wèi kèhù)/ 一个客户(yí gè kèhù)	A client
老板(lǎobǎn)	个(gè)	一个老板(yí gè lǎobǎn)	A boss
名片(míngpiàn)	张(zhāng)/ 盒(hé)/ 沓(dá)	一张名片(yì zhāng míngpiàn)	A visiting card
软盘(ruǎnpán)	张(zhāng)	一张软盘(yì zhāng ruǎnpán)	A floppy disk
市场(shìchǎng)	个(gè)	一个市场(yí gè shìchǎng)	A market
照片(zhàopiān)	张(zhāng)	一张照片(yì zhāng zhàopiān)	A photo
茶(chá)	杯(bēi)/ 壶(hú)	一杯茶(yì bēi chá)/ 一壶茶(yì hú chá)	A cup of tea A pot of tea

咖啡(kāfēi)	杯(bēi)/ 壶(hú)	一杯咖啡(yì bēi kāfēi)/ 一壶咖啡(yì hú kāfēi)	A cup of coffee, a pot of coffee
牛奶(niúnǎi)	杯(bēi) / 瓶(píng)/ 盒(hé)	一杯牛奶(yì bēi niúnǎi)/ 一瓶牛奶(yì píng niúnǎi)/ 一盒牛奶(yì hé niúnǎi)	A glass of milk, a bottle of milk, a box of milk

练 习 Exercises

一、请听录音或跟着老师读。

Listen to the recording or read after the teacher.

duī → d uī → duī
duì → d uì → duì

guān → g uān → guān
guǎn → g uǎn → guǎn
guàn → g uàn → guàn

dū → d ū → dū
dú → d ú → dú
dǔ → d ǔ → dǔ
dù → d ù → dù

lē → l ē → lē
lè → l è → lè

méi → m éi → méi
měi → m ěi → měi
mèi → m èi → mèi

xī → x ī → xī
xí → x í → xí
xǐ → x ǐ → xǐ
xì → x ì → xì

chē → ch ē → chē
chě → ch ě → chě
chè → ch è → chè

liāo → l iāo → liāo
liáo → l iáo → liáo
liǎo → l iǎo → liǎo
liào → l iào → liào

二、听录音并熟读下面的句子。

Listen to the recording and read the following sentences till you learn them by heart.

1. Duìbuqǐ.
对不起！

2. Dǔ chē le.
堵 车 了。

3. Méi guānxi.
没 关系。

4. Zhēn duìbuqǐ!
真 对不起！

三、跟读并辨别下面音节。

Read the following syllables and try to tell one from the other.

dǔchē—bǔzhuō
zīliào—chīyào
zhēnhǎo—zhènghǎo
guānxì—guānxīn

四、请让我们一起再学习几个常用的词语，然后做练习。

Learn more useful words before you do the exercise.

补充词语 Supplementary Words

晚	wǎn	(形)	late	*(adj.)*
抱歉	bàoqiàn	(动)	sorry	*(v.)*
没事儿	méi shìr		not serious, never mind	
不要紧	bú yàojǐn		It doesn't matter.	

选择填空 Fill in the Blanks with Appropriate Words

duìbuqǐ(对不起) méi guānxi(没关系)

lái wǎng le(来晚了) bàoqiàn(抱歉)

1.A：Màizǒng, duìbuqǐ, lái wǎn le.
A：麦总， 对不起， 来 晚 了。
B：________________________。

2.A：Zhēn duìbuqǐ!
A： 真 对不起！__________。
B：Méi shìr.
B：没 事儿。

3.A：Hěn
A：很________________________。
B：Bú yàojǐn.
B：不 要紧。

4.A：Zhēn zhèige chuánzhēn sòng wǎn le.
A：真______，这个 传真 送（deliver）晚 了。
B：________________________。

五、请在下面括号中添上适当的量词。

Fill the brackets with appropriate measure words.

一（ ）传真
三（ ）电脑
五（ ）纸
七（ ）书
六（ ）桌子

六、把下面表达相同意思的汉字、拼音、英文用线连起来。

Connect the equivalent sentences in *pinyin*, characters and English in the three columns with a line.

A.对不起!	1.Zhēn duìbuqǐ!	(1) Caught in a traffic jam.
B.堵车了。	2.Méi guānxi.	(2) Awfully sorry!
C.没关系。	3.Duìbuqǐ!	(3) Sorry!
D.真对不起!	4.Dǔ chē le.	(4) Never mind.

七、下面的情景用汉语你知道该怎么说吗？请试一试。

Try to express yourself in the following situations.

1.当你不小心踩了别人脚的时候，你应该赶紧对他说什么?
How do you apologize in Chinese for accidentally trampling on someone's toes?

2.当你从同事的旁边经过时，把他的书碰掉了，你赶快向他道歉。
How do you apologize in Chinese to your colleague for accidentally knocking his book down when you pass by?

3.你的客户对你提出产品质量问题时，你首先对他说什么道歉的话?
How will you apologize in Chinese for the bad quality of your products your customer is complaining about?

八、汉字点击。

Open the CD to view the characters.

请通过光盘点击认读、书写下面的汉字。请注意汉字书写时的笔顺。

Open the CD, click on the buttons, read and write the following characters, paying attention to their stroke-order.

对 起 没 关 系 堵 车 了 资 料 呢 里

自我评估 Self-assessment

1.学会了这么多汉语句子，你在中国的生活是否感觉方便一些了?
Do you feel more convenient about your life in China after you have learned so many Chinese sentences?

2.学习这一课你用了多长时间？

How much time have you spent in learning this text?

3.你是否已经喜欢上汉语了？

Do you like learning the Chinese language now?

文化点击 Cultural Points

中国人的道歉　Chinese apologies

中国人在打扰、影响别人，或给别人带来麻烦的时候要说“对不起！”“抱歉！”的话，比如不小心弄坏了别人的东西，无意中碰掉了别人的物品，没注意踩了别人的脚，赴约晚到等等，都需要说“对不起！”或者“真对不起！”“很抱歉！”但是请求帮助时，比如问路时就不用先说“对不起”。

Chinese people say “I beg your pardon” or “sorry” for having done wrong, having disturbed people or having caused trouble. The apologetic expressions of “duìbuqǐ”(sorry), “zhēn duìbuqǐ”(awfully sorry and)“hěn bàoqiàn” (pardon me) are applicable to, for example, accidental damage, trampling on one's toes or breaking an appointment. However it is unnecessary to say “duìbuqǐ” before one asks the way.

Dì-shí kè Wǒ néng yòng zhèige diànnǎo ma
第10课 我能用这个电脑吗
Lesson 10 May I Use This Computer

导学 Guiding Remarks

在很多场合，我们想做某件事情的时候需要征得他人同意。本课我们将学习汉语中几句客气的说法，你可以用这些话请求他人允许你做你想做的事。

At times we cannot do anything without permission. In this lesson we will learn a few Chinese sentences for asking permission to do something.

课文 Text

A

John comes to the office where Li Lin works.

John：Lǐ Lín，wǒ néng yòng yíxià zhèige diànnǎo ma?
John：李琳，我　能　用　一下　这个　电脑　吗？
John：Li Lin，may I use this computer?

Lǐ Lín：Yòng ba.
李　琳：用　吧。
Li Lin：Yes，you can.

John：Wǒ kěyǐ yòng zhèige ruǎnpán ma?
John：我　可以　用　这个　软盘　吗？
John：May I use this floppy disk?

Lǐ Lín：Kěyǐ.
李　琳：可以。
Li Lin：Yes，you can.

John：Xièxie!
John：谢谢！
John：Thanks.

B

A customer knocks at the door, then pushes it open into Mike's office.

Kèhù：Wǒ kěyǐ jìnlái ma?
客户：我 可以 进来 吗？
Customer：May I come in?

Màikè：Qǐng jìn.
麦克：请 进。
Mike：Come in，please.

Kèhù：Nín hǎo! Wǒ kěyǐ gěi nín tí yì diǎn yìjiàn ma?
客户：您 好！我 可以 给 您 提 一 点 意见 吗？
Customer：Good morning! Can I make some suggestions to you?

Màikè：Hǎo, qǐng tí.
麦克：好，请 提。
Mike：Sure，just go ahead.

词 语 Word List

1.能	néng	(动)	can, to be able	(v.)
2.吗	ma	(语气)	(a final interrogative particle)	(mp.)
3.吧	ba	(语气)	(a modal particle)	(mp.)
4.软盘	ruǎnpán	(名)	software	(n.)
5.进来	jìnlái	(动)	to come in	(v.)
6.提	tí	(动)	to propose, to make	(v.)
7.意见	yìjiàn	(名)	suggestion, comment, complaint	(n.)

语言点链接 Language Points

"能"和"可以" The usage of "néng" and "kěyǐ"

出现在动词前面的"能"、"可以"的特点是：

(1)可以放在动词的前面，如"能来、能提意见、可以进、可以坐"等。

(2)可以单独回答问题，如"我可以进来吗？——可以"。

(3)可以在前面加"不"表示否定，如"我能进来吗？——不能／不可以"。

当表示允许做某件事时，"能"和"可以"的用法是一样的。本课的"我能进来吗？"意思是请求听话人允许说话人进来，这时候也可以说："我可以进来吗？"回答都是"可以"或"不可以"，而不是"能"或"不能"。"能"还有一个意思，是表示某件事是否有实现的条件，所以这时候"我能进来吗"的意思可能是"门太小，我不知道我这么胖的身体是否能通过"，回答是"能"或者"不能"，而不能回答"可以"或"不可以"。

同类的词语还有"要、应该、会、能够、可能"等。

The characteristics of pre-verbal "néng" and "kěyǐ" are：

a. They can be placed before verbs as in "néng lái", "néng tí yìjiàn", "kěyǐ jìn", "kěyǐ zuò".

b. They can stand by themselves in reply to a question. E.g. "wǒ néng jìnlái ma" —— "kěyǐ".

c. They can be preceded by "bù" to indicate the negation. E.g. "wǒ kěyǐ jìnlái ma" —— "bù néng" / "bù kěyǐ".

Both "néng" andg "kěyǐ" can be used to indicate the permission. "wǒ néng jìnlái ma" is equal to "wǒ kěyǐ jìnlái ma" meaning "May I come in?" The answers to both questions are never "néng" or "bù néng", but "kěyǐ" or "bù kěyǐ". "néng" also suggests "possibility". In "wǒ néng jìnlái ma" the understatement is "Is the door wide enough for a fat man like me to get through?" In this case the answer expected is "néng" or "bù néng", instead of "kěyǐ" or "bù kěyǐ".

There are some more optative verbs such as "yào", "yīnggāi", "huì", "nénggòu" and "kěnéng" etc...

练 习 Exercises

一、请听录音或跟着老师读。

Listen to the recording or read after the teacher.

néng → n éng → néng

nāo → n āo → nāo
náo → n áo → náo
nǎo → n ǎo → nǎo
nào → n ào → nào

bā → b ā → bā
bá → b á → bá
bǎ → b ǎ → bǎ
bà → b à → bà

pān → p ān → pān
pán → p án → pán
pàn → p àn → pàn

hū → h ū → hū
hú → h ú → hú
hǔ → h ǔ → hǔ
hù → h ù → hù

xiāng → x iāng → xiāng
xiáng → x iáng → xiáng
xiǎng → x iǎng → xiǎng
xiàng → x iàng → xiàng

diān → d iān → diān
diǎn → d iǎn → diǎn
diàn → d iàn → diàn

mā → m ā → mā
má → m á → má
mǎ → m ǎ → mǎ
mà → m à → mà

ruán → r uán → ruán
ruǎn → r uǎn → ruǎn

kē → k ē → kē
ké → k é → ké
kě → k ě → kě
kè → k è → kè

lái → l ái → lái
lài → l ài → lài

tī → t ī → tī
tí → t í → tí
tǐ → t ǐ → tǐ
tì → t ì → tì

jiān → j　iān → jiān
jiǎn → j　iǎn → jiǎn
jiàn → j　iàn → jiàn

二、听录音并熟读下面的句子。

Listen to the recording, read the following sentences till you learn them by heart.

1. Wǒ néng yòng yíxià zhèige diànnǎo ma?
我　能　用　一下　这个　电脑　吗?

2. Yòng ba.
用　吧。

3. Wǒ kěyǐ yòng zhèige ruǎnpán ma?
我　可以　用　这个　软盘　吗?

4. Kěyǐ.
可以。

5. Wǒ kěyǐ jìnlái ma?
我　可以　进来　吗?

6. Wǒ kěyǐ gěi nín tí yì diǎn yìjiàn ma?
我　可以　给　您　提　一　点　意见　吗?

三、跟读并辨别下面音节。

Read the following syllables after the teacher and try to tell one from the other.

kěyǐ–hétǐ
diànnǎo–dàjiǎo
ruǎnpán–yǎnyuán
yìjiàn–yíbiàn

四、请让我们一起再学习几个常用的词语，然后做练习。

Learn more useful words before you do the exercises.

补充词语 Supplementary Words

行	xíng	(动)	O.K., fine	*(v.)*
抽烟	chōu yān		to smoke	
随便	suíbiàn	(形)	as you like, casual	*(adj.)*

选择填空 Fill in the Blanks with Appropriate Words

diànnǎo(电脑)　　xíng(行)　　kěyǐ(可以)

1. A: Xiǎojiě, wǒ ______ chōu yān ma?
   A: 小姐， 我______________抽 烟 吗?
   B: Suíbiàn.
   B: 随便。

2. A: Lǐ Lín, nǐ néng lái yíxià ma?
   A: 李 琳, 你 能 来 一下 吗?
   B: ____________________________。

3. A: Wǒ néng yòng nǐde ______ ma?
   A: 我 能 用 你的__________吗?
   B: Yòng ba.
   B: 用 吧。

4. A: Wǒ kěyǐ fā yí gē chuánzhēn ma?
   A: 我 可以 发 一 个 传真 吗?
   B: ____________________________。

五、把下面的汉字试着加上拼音.

Add *pinyin* into the following characters into pinyin.

能　软　盘　客　户　来

六、把下面表达相同意思的汉字、拼音、英文用线连起来。

Connect the equivalent sentences in *pinyin*, characters and English in the three columns with a line.

A. 用吧。	1. Wǒ kěyǐ jìnlái ma?	(1) Yes, you can.
B. 可以。	2. Yòng ba.	(2) May I come in?
C. 我可以进来吗?	3. Kěyǐ.	(3) Sure.

七、下面的情景用汉语你知道该怎么说吗？请试一试。

Try to express yourself in the following situations.

1. 你来到一个公司应聘，先敲门，然后用汉语提出请求进屋。
   How will you request to come into an office for an interview in Chinese when you apply for a post?

2. 现在有人请求借你的车一用，你愿意借给他，请用汉语告诉他。
   Tell the borrower in Chinese that you agree to lend your car to him.

3. 你去商场买东西，你希望试穿一下衣服，用汉语对售货员提出请求。
   Ask the shop assistant in Chinese if you can try on the garment that you wish to buy.

八、汉字点击。

Open the CD to view the characters.

请通过光盘点击认读、书写下面的汉字。请注意汉字书写时的笔顺。

Open the CD, click the buttons, read and write the following Chinese characters, focusing your attention on their stroke-order.

能　脑　吗　吧　软　盘　客　户　来　提　意　见

自我评估 Self-assessment

1. 你感觉用汉语请别人帮忙难吗？
   Is it difficult for you to ask a favour of someone in Chinese?

2.你在学习本课后，自己还想到了什么相关句子？
Are there any other sentences related to the subject that you have found after learning the present text?

3.中国人表达请求时的话容易学吗？
Are the Chinese expressions for request easy to learn?

文化点击 Cultural Points

公休与作息制度 General holidays and daily schedule

中国的公休日有下面的几个：星期六和星期日休息，新年放1天假，春节放3天假，“五一”劳动节（5月1日）放3天假，“十一”国庆节（10月1日）放3天假。现在实行黄金周制度，即，春节、“五一”、“十一”时都把相邻的双休日换过来，这样就可以连续休息7天。

中国的劳动制度每周工作5天，一般是每天工作8小时，大多数是早8：00或9：00到中午12点工作，下午1：00或2：00到晚上5：00或6：00工作。中国人大多有午睡的习惯，所以有很多单位中午休息时间是两个小时。

General holidays in China are Saturday, Sunday, New Year's day (one day off), the Spring Festival (three days off), Labour Day (May 1st, three days off) and the National Day (October 1st, three days off). What is known as the Golden Weeks includes the Spring Festival, May 1st and October 1st on which people take seven days off by connecting two weekends and the holidays together.

Under the Chinese system people work for eight hours daily and five days weekly. The working hours are arranged between 8 (or 9) to 12 am, and 1 (or 2) to 5 (or 6) pm. Many people take an afternoon nap, therefore the lunch break in many companies can be as long as two hours.

Dì-shíyī kè　Bú yòng le
第 11 课　不用了
Lesson 11　Oh, No, Thanks Anyway

导学 Guiding Remarks

生活中你可能会遇到自己不愿意做或不愿意接受的事，如何拒绝而不使双方尴尬，这可是一门语言的艺术。下面几句话，会对你有所帮助的。

From day to day we are bound to encounter problems of dissatisfaction and or things we dislike. It is an art of language to refuse someone without hurting his/her feelings. The following sentences may be useful as a solution to your dilemma.

课文 Text

A

During the coffee break Li Lin goes to the office carrying a whole pile of sample products. Wang Guang sees her on his way down to the coffee bar.

Wáng Guāng：Yào bú yào wǒ bāng máng？
王 光：要 不要 我 帮 忙？
Wang Guang：Can I help you?

Lǐ Lín：Bú yòng le.
李 琳：不 用 了。
Li Lin：Oh，No，It's O.K.

Wáng Guāng：Bié kè qi.
王 光：别 客气。(Extending his hand)
Wang Guang：There's no need for ceremony.

Lǐ Lín：Bú yòng，bú yòng. Zhēn de bú yòng.
李 琳：不 用，不 用。真 的 不 用。
Li Lin：Don't bother，really. I can manage myself.

B

Wang Guang is sitting in the coffee bar.

Fúwùyuán: Kāfēi jiā nǎi ma?
服务员：咖啡 加 奶 吗？
Waiter: White coffee, sir?

Wáng Guāng: Bú yòng.
王 光：不 用。
Wang Guang: Oh, No, No milk.

Fúwùyuán: Jiā táng ma?
服务员：加 糖 吗？
Waiter: What about sugar?

Wáng Guāng: Bú yòng, xièxie!
王 光：不 用， 谢谢！
Wang Guang: Oh, No, No sugar, please. Thanks!

词 语 Word List

1.要	yào	(动)	to want, to need	*(v.)*
2.帮忙	bāng máng		help	
3.别	bié	(副)	do not	*(adv.)*
4.咖啡	kāfēi	(名)	coffee	*(n.)*
5.加	jiā	(动)	to add to	*(v.)*
6.奶	nǎi	(名)	milk	*(n.)*

语言点链接 Language Points

1.疑问句(yí wènjù) Interrogative sentences

汉语的疑问句有4种：

(1) 在句末加“吗、吧”等疑问词，后面加问号（?）的形式。例如：“你好吗？”“你明白了吧？”等等。

(2) 用"什么、哪儿、怎么"等疑问词来发问，句末加问号（?）的形式。例如"你什么时候去？""你从哪儿来？""你怎么了？"等等。

(3) 用动词或形容词的肯定和否定形式连接起来表示疑问，后面加问号（?）的形式。例如："房间大不大？""你来不来？""中餐好吃不好吃？"等等。

(4) 用"要、可以、能"等能愿动词的肯定和否定形式连接起来表示疑问，后面加问号（?）的形式。例如"你要不要帮忙？""他能不能来？""你可以不可以来一下?"等等。

There are four types of interrogative sentences in Chinese:

a. A statement followed by "ma" or "ba" together with a question mark functions as an interrogative sentence. e.g. "nǐ hǎo ma?" "nǐ míngbái le ba?"

b. An interrogative pronoun such as "shénme", "nǎr", "zěnme" and a question mark can be used to form an interrogative sentence. E.g. "nǐ shénme shíhou qù?" "nǐ cóng nǎr lái?" and "nǐ zěnme le?"

c. The affirmative and negative form of a verb or an adjective together with a question mark can be used to form an interrogative sentence. E.g. "fángjiān dà bú dà?" "nǐ lái bù lái?" and "zhōngcān hǎo chī bù hǎo chī?"

d. An affirmative and negative form of the optative verbs "yào", "kěyǐ" or "néng" plus a question mark can be used to form an interrogative sentence. E.g. "nǐ yào bú yào bāng máng?" "tā néng bù néng lái?" and "nǐ kěyǐ bù kěyǐ lái yí xià?"

2. 汉语常用的标点符号简介 Commonly used Chinese Punctuation Marks

名称 Marks	拼音 *Pinyin*	用法 Usage	英文 English
句号（。）	jù hào	用在陈述句末尾。	full stop
逗号（，）	dòu hào	用在一句话中间的停顿处。	comma
顿号（、）	dùn hào	用在句中较短的停顿处。	slight-pause mark
问号（？）	wèn hào	用在问句末尾。	question mark
感叹号（！）	gǎntàn hào	用在表达强烈感情的句末。	exclamation mark
分号（；）	fēn hào	用在并列的分句组中间。	semicolon
省略号（……）	shěnglüè hào	用在文中省略部分处。	ellipsis dots
破折号（——）	pòzhé hào	表示话题的转换，或者表示后面有注释性部分。	dash
引号（" "）	yǐn hào	用在引用别人原句的前后。	quotation marks
冒号（：）	mào hào	用在提示下文的提示语后。	colon
括号（（））	kuò hào	用在对前面作解释或注释的语句的前后。	brackets
书名号（《》、〈〉）	shūmíng hào	用在书籍、报刊、文章等作品的名称前后。	marks for titles of book, newspapers, articles etc.

着重号（.）	zhuózhòng hào	用在需要强调的语句的下面。	mark of emphasis
间隔号（·）	jiāngé hào	用在日期、音译姓名等中间。	separation dot
连接号（—）	lián zì hào	用在两个有联系的词语中间。	hyphen

练　习　Exercises

一、请听录音或跟着老师读。

Listen to the recording or read after the teacher.

yāo → y　āo → yāo
yáo → y　áo → yáo
yǎo → y　ǎo → yǎo
yào → y　ào → yào

gěi → g　ěi → gěi

kā → k　ā → kā
kǎ → k　ǎ → kǎ

biē → b　iē → biē
bié → b　ié → bié
biě → b　iě → biě
biè → b　iè → biè

fēi → f　ēi → fēi
féi → f　éi → féi
fěi → f　ěi → fěi
fèi → f　èi → fèi

shōu → sh　ōu → shōu
shóu → sh　óu → shóu
shǒu → sh　ǒu → shǒu
shòu → sh　òu → shòu

huō → h　uō → huō
huó → h　uó → huó
huǒ → h　uǒ → huǒ
huò → h　uò → huò

nǎi → n　ǎi → nǎi
nài → n　ài → nài

tāng → t　āng → tāng
táng → t　áng → táng
tǎng → t　ǎng → tǎng
tàng → t　àng → tàng

二、听录音并熟读下面的句子。

Listen to the recording and read the following sentences till you learn them by heart.

1. Yào bú yào wǒ bāng máng?
   要 不 要 我 帮 忙?

2. Bú yòng le.
   不 用 了。

3. Kāfēi jiā nǎi ma?
   咖啡 加 奶 吗?

4. Jiā táng ma?
   加 糖 吗?

三、跟读并辨别下面音节。

Read the following syllables after the teacher and try to tell one from the other.

kāfēi–kāihuì　　　búyòng–bútòng
gěinǐ–měinǚ　　　jiātáng–jiācháng

四、请让我们一起再学习几个常用的词语，然后做练习。

Learn more useful words before you do the exercises.

补充词语 Supplementary Words

需要　xūyào　（动）　to need　*(v.)*

选择填空 Fill in the Blanks with Appropriate Words

bāng máng(帮忙)　　　　bú yòng le(不用了)

1. A：Xiǎo Wáng，xūyào wǒ bāng máng ma?
   A：小 王，需要 我 帮 忙 吗?
   B：____________________________。

2.A：Kāfēi jiā nǎi ma?
A：咖啡 加 奶 吗?
B：______________。

3.A：Yòng bú yòng wǒ
A：用　不 用 我__________?
B：Bú yòng le. Xièxie!
B：不　用　了。谢 谢!

五、试着给下面的句子加上标点。

Add punctuation marks to the following sentences.

1. Yòng wǒ bāng máng ma
用 我 帮 忙 吗

2. Gěi gōngsī fā yí gè chuánzhēn
给 公司 发 一 个 传真

3. Wǒ kěyǐ bù kěyǐ yòng nǐ de diànnǎo
我 可以 不 可以 用 你 的 电脑

4. Kāfēi yòng bú yòng jiā táng
咖啡 用 不 用 加 糖

六、把下面表达相同意思的汉字、拼音、英文用线连起来。

Connect the equivalent sentences in *pinyin*, characters and English in the three columns with a line.

A.要不要我帮忙?	1. Bú yòng le.	(1) Oh, no.
B.不用了。	2. Kāfēi jiā táng ma?	(2) Can I help you?
C.咖啡加糖吗?	3. Yào bú yào wǒ bāng máng?	(3) Can I put sugar into your coffee?

七、下面的情景用汉语你知道该怎么说吗?请试一试。

Try to express yourself in the following situations.

1. 当你看到别人的车有了问题时，你很想帮他忙，请你用汉语热心地问一下。
How will you express yourself in Chinese when you want to help a man fix his car?

2. 你的中国朋友的生意不太景气，他正在发愁时，你去关心一下他。
How will you console your Chinese friend when he is anxious for his ailing business?

3.当你有了困难，别人想帮助你时，请你用汉语婉言谢绝。

Decline an offer in Chinese when someone wants to help you out of difficulty.

八、汉字点击。

Open the CD to view the characters.

请通过光盘点击认读、书写下面的汉字。请注意汉字书写时的笔顺。

Open the CD, click the buttons, read and write the following Chinese characters, focusing your attention on their stroke-order.

要　别　咖　啡　售　货　加　奶　糖

自我评估 Self-assessment

1.学会本课的几句话你用了多长时间?

How long did it take you to learn the sentences in the text?

2.在别人需要帮助时,你是否可以用汉语来对他表示你愿意帮助他?

Can you express yourself in Chinese when you wish to help someone overcome his difficulties?

3.你认为汉语中婉言谢绝的句子难吗?

Are the Chinese expressions for declining difficult for you to learn?

文化点击 Cultural Points

"不用"就是不需要帮助吗? Does "bú yòng" only mean one's refusal?

当你想给中国人提供某种帮助的时候，即使他真的需要帮助，他可能也先说"不用了"。

但是如果你认为他真的需要帮助，你就要继续表示你愿意帮忙，这时他可能会说"不好意思"、"麻烦你了"，表示他接受了。如果他确实不需要帮助的话，他会继续拒绝。

"bú yòng le" may be used to avoid bothering someone. If you think your help is necessary, you'd better insist on your offer. Then your assistance is likely to be accepted with a "bù hǎo yìsi"(sorry to trouble you), "máfan nǐ le" (sorry to bother you), which implies that your offer is appreciated. If one feels it unnecessary to bother anybody, one will decline further.

Dì-shí'èr kè　Nín xiān qǐng
第 12 课　您 先 请
Lesson 12　After You

导学 Guiding Remarks

中国人有谦让的传统美德，到中国你也应该学会用中国话表示谦让。下面的课文就是谦让的场景。注意他们是怎么说的。

Traditionally giving precedence to others out of courtesy is regarded as exhibiting one's moral excellence in China. This topic is to be covered in this lesson. The sentences given below are often used in such situations.

A

Having finished the office routine for the day, the employees, together with Mike, are waiting for the lift. Now the door is open, they give precedence to one another.

A：Màizǒng，nín xiān qǐng!
A：麦总，　您　先　请!
A：Maizong，please!

Màikè：　　Nǐmen xiān shàng.
麦克：(politely) 你们　先　上。
Mike：After you.

A：Nín qǐng xiān shàng!
A：您　请　先　上!
A：After you, sir!

B：Màizǒng nín qǐng!
B：麦总　您　请!
B：Maizong, please!

C：Nín qǐng!
C：您　请!
C：Please, sir!

Màikè：Bié kèqi. Háishì nǐmen xiān shàng.
麦克：别 客气。还是 你们　先　上。
Mike：Don't stand on ceremony. Age after beauty!

They all refuse to be the first when the lift noisily leaves the laughing employees behind.

B

Mike，John and Li Lin are having their meal at the canteen. John pours the tea for Li Lin next to him, but Li insists on being served later. Mike is opposite to John.

Lǐ Lín：Nǐ xiān lái.
李　琳：你　先　来。
Li Lin：After you.

John：Bié kèqi.
John：别　客气。Ladies first.
John：No need to be so formal.

Lǐ Lín：Bié，Màizǒng xiān lái ba.
李　琳：别，　麦总　先　来吧。
Li Lin：No，Maizong, after you.

Màikè：Bù，bù，háishì nǐ xiān lái.
麦克：不，不，还是　你　先　来。
Mike：No,no, I insist on serving you first.

John：Qǐng!
John：(Starting to pour the tea for Li Lin)请!
John：For you!

Lǐ Lín：Xièxie!
李　琳：谢谢!
Li Lin：Thank you!

John wants to help Mike with the tea, but he finds it difficult to reach the cup, so he has to stand up.

Màikē: Wǒ zìjǐ lái.
麦克：(Extending his hand for the teapot) 我 自己 来。
Mike：Let me do it myself.

John： Wǒ lái, wǒ lái. Nǐ shì lǎobǎn.
John：(Holding the teapot firmly) 我 来，我 来。你 是 老板。
John：Let me serve you. You are my boss.

Màikē：Xièxie!
麦克：谢谢! (Gladly giving him the cup) It's my pleasure to be attended to, but I have no small change for the tip at the moment.
Mike：Thank you!

词语 Word List

1.先	xiān	(副)	first	*(adv.)*
2.上	shàng	(动)	to go up	*(v.)*
3.还是	háishì	(副)	had better, still	*(adv.)*
4.来	lái	(动)	to let	*(v.)*
4.自己	zìjǐ	(代)	oneself	*(pron.)*
5.老板	lǎobǎn	(名)	boss	*(n.)*

语言点链接 Language Points

"来" The usage of "lái"

"来"本来的意思是表示向着说话者方向移动的动作。但有的时候还可以代指做某个动作或者事情，如本课中的"你先来"，就是指"先给你倒茶。"麦克说"我自己来"，是说"我自己倒茶"。比方说你的电脑出现了问题，你的同事在旁边给你指点，这时你站起来，手指坐位对他说："你来，你来。"在这里，"来"的意思就表示"请坐这里帮助我解决电脑故障"的意思。

In addition to the implication of one's movement towards the speaker, "lái" also stands for one's action. E.g. "nǐ xiān lái" (serve you with the tea first) and "wǒ zìjǐ lái" (I'll do it myself). Supposing your computer is out of order, and your colleague shows how to fix it, you may say "nǐ lái, nǐ lái" (Please take the seat and help me with the trouble solved.)

练　习　Exercises

一、请听录音或跟着老师读。

Listen to the recording or read after the teacher.

xiān → x　iān → xiān
xián → x　ián → xián
xiǎn → x　iǎn → xiǎn
xiàn → x　iàn → xiàn

hāi → h　āi → hāi
hái → h　ái → hái
hǎi → h　ǎi → hǎi
hài → h　ài → hài

lāo → l　āo → lāo
láo → l　áo → láo
lǎo → l　ǎo → lǎo
lào → l　ào → lào

wēi → w　ēi → wēi
wéi → w　éi → wéi
wěi → w　ěi → wěi
wèi → w　èi → wèi

shāng → sh　āng → shāng
shǎng → sh　ǎng → shǎng
shàng → sh　àng → shàng

jī → j　ī → jī
jí → j　í → jí
jǐ → j　ǐ → jǐ
jì → j　ì → jì

bān → b　ān → bān
bǎn → b　ǎn → bǎn
bàn → b　àn → bàn

二、听录音并熟读下面的句子。

Listen to the recording and read the following sentences till you learn them by heart.

1. Nín xiān qǐng.
您 先 请。

2. Nín qǐng xiān shàng.
您 请 先 上。

3. Bié kèqi. Háishì nǐmen xiān shàng.
别 客气。还是 你们 先 上。

4. Wǒ zìjǐ lái.
我 自己 来。

5. Nǐ shì lǎobǎn.
你 是 老板。

三、跟读并辨别下面音节。

Read the following syllables and try to tell one from the other.

lǎobǎn—náwǎn
zìjǐ—zhījǐ
háishì—fèishì
wǒlái—wèilái

四、请让我们一起再学习几个常用的词语，然后做练习。

Learn more useful words before you do the exercises.

补充词语 Supplementary Words

走	zǒu	(动)	to go, to walk	(v.)
下	xià	(动)	to go down	(v.)

选择填空 Fill in the Blanks with Appropriate Words

qǐng(请)　　xiān(先)　　shàng(上)

1.A：Jīnglǐ,nín xiān zǒu.

A：经理，您 先 走。

B：Nǐ xiān

B：你 先 ____________。

2.A：Lǐ Lín,nǐ xiān xià ba.

A：李 琳，你 先 下 吧。

B：Nǐ　　　　　　　xià.

B：你 ____________ 下。

3.A：Màizǒng,nín xiān

A：麦总，您 先 ________。

B：Nǐ xiān shàng ba.

B：你 先 上 吧。

4.A：Nín xiān qǐng.

A：您 先 请。

B：Bù,nín

B：不，您 ____________。

五、请仔细体会下面句子里“来”的意思。

Carefully study the usage of “lái” in the following sentences.

1.Màizǒng lái le.

麦总　来了。

2.Qǐng jìnlái ba.

请　进来 吧。

3.　　Wǒ lái, wǒ lái.

(When you are going to pay for the meal) 我 来，我 来。

4.　　Nǐ xiān lái.

(When you are queueing for food) 你 先 来。

六、把下面表达相同意思的汉字、拼音、英文用线连起来。

Connect the equivalent sentences in *pinyin*, characters and English in the three columns with a line.

A.您请先上。	1. Bié kèqi.	(1) Don't stand on ceremony
B.我自己来。	2. Wǒ zìjǐ lái.	(2) After you.
C.别客气。	3. Nín qǐng xiān shàng.	(3) Let me do it myself.

七、下面的情景用汉语你知道该怎么说吗？请试一试。

Try to express yourself in the following situations.

1.在公共汽车站，你的旁边是一位老年人，汽车来了，你客气地对他表示谦让。
You ask an old man to get on the bus first when the bus arrives at the bus stop.

2.你和同事一起进公司大门时，你怎样跟同事表示谦让？
You say "after you" in Chinese to your colleagues at the gate of the company.

3.你和朋友在饭店吃饭时，菜上来了，你对朋友说什么？
You ask your friends to start the meal in Chinese when dishes are being served on the table in a restaurant.

八、汉字点击。

Open the CD to view the characters.

请通过光盘点击认读、书写下面的汉字。请注意汉字书写时的笔顺。

Open the CD, read and write the following characters with special attention to their stroke-order.

先　上　还　自　己　老　板　为

自我评估 Self-assessment

1.你习惯中国人的谦让吗？
What do you think of the Chinese way of giving people precedence out of courtesy?

2.本课几句表示谦让的话你都能用好吗？

Are you able to use the sentences inviting precedence provided in the text?

3.学习本课你用了多长时间？

How long did it take you to learn the text?

文化点击 Cultural Points

中国人的礼让　Precedence and Courtesy

中国人在很多场合都要表示谦让，特别是对尊长更要礼让。当中国人对你表示谦让时，你最好不要直接接受，也要谦让一下。比如，在进门的时候，别人请你先走，你最好不要先走，而应该请对方先走，否则给人感觉你很不客气。在同桌就餐时（不是分餐），中国人总是要等到尊长先动筷子。但是请你记住，在付账的时候，中国人是决不礼让的，他们都尽量争抢去付。

Chinese people often give precedence to one another, especially according to seniority, in social communication. It is advisable for one to decline an offer if one can. Supposing someone asks one to go first at an entrance, one may insist on him/her taking the precedence. If not, one doesn't seem to have good manners. It also applies to table behaviour. Guests, especially aged members, are always invited to start a meal first. However Chinese participants will invariably try to be the first to pay the bill.

Dì-shísān kè　Nǐ zhēn xíng
第 13 课　你真行
Lesson 13　You Are Really Terrific

导学 Guiding Remarks

别人取得了成就，我们都要对他表示赞赏和夸奖；当我们看到美好的事物时，我们也常常发出一些赞叹。学完本课，你就可以掌握几句常用的夸奖和赞叹的话。

We express our praise for someone's success, and are lost in the admiration of beautiful things. In this lesson you will learn how to make complimentary remarks in Chinese.

A

Li Lin shows her colleagues a chart of employees' monthly achievements in which Wang Guang is listed top. Mike compliments Wang as he passes.

Màikè: Xiǎo Wáng, bú cuò a!
麦克：小　王，不 错 啊！
Mike: Well done, Xiao Wang.

Wáng Guāng: Guòjiǎng le.
王 光：过奖　了。
Wang Guang: You flatter me.

The employees successively come to the office. Upon seeing the chart they praise and congratulate Wang Guang on his achievements.

Tóngshì A: Xiǎo Wáng, nǐ zhēn xíng!
同事A：小　王，你 真　行！(clapping with him.)
Colleague A: Xiao Wang, you are really terrific!

Tóngshì B: Xiǎo Wáng, qǐng kè a!
同事B：小　王，　请　客啊！(Patting him on the shoulder.)
Colleague B: Xiao Wang, are you going to treat us to a drink?

Wáng Guāng: Hǎo!
王 光：好！
Wang Guang: Yes, I am.

B

The employees are talking about a newly-designed poster.

Lǐ Lín：Bú cuò, hěn hǎo.
李琳：不 错，很 好。
Li Lin：Oh, that's great.

Wáng Guāng：Huàmiàn hěn měi. Shēngyīn yě bú cuò.
王光：画面　很 美。 声音　也不 错。
Wang Guang：The picture is really beautiful, and the sound is good too.

John：Hěn hǎo. Wǒ xǐhuan.
John：很 好。 我 喜欢。
John：Gorgeous, I like it.

词　语　Word List

1.行	xíng	（形）	fine	*(adj.)*
2.不错	bú cuò	（形）	not bad	*(adj.)*
3.过奖	guòjiǎng	（动）	to overpraise	*(v.)*
4.请	qǐng	（动）	to entertain, to invite	*(v.)*
5.请客	qǐng kè		to stand treat	
6.画面	huàmiàn	（名）	picture	*(n.)*
7.美	měi	（形）	beautiful	*(adj.)*
8.声音	shēngyīn	（名）	sound	*(n.)*
9.喜欢	xǐhuan	（动）	to like	*(v.)*

语言点链接　Language Points

“行” The usage of “xíng”

“行”在汉语中表示同意时的应答，意思同“可以”或“好吧”。如“你能帮我个忙吗？——行。”当表示赞赏时，意思同“好”，一般用为“你真行!”表示赞赏别人做得好。

“xíng”, equal to “kěyǐ” or “hǎo ba”, is used to indicate one’s agreement as in “nǐ néng bāng wǒ gè máng ma” —— “xíng”. It also means “good” or “capable” as in the complimentary remark “nǐ zhēn xíng”.

练　习　Exercises

一、请听录音或跟着老师读。

Listen to the recording or read after the teacher.

cuō → c　uō → cuō　　　dī → d　ī → dī
cuó → c　uó → cuó　　　dí → d　í → dí
cuǒ → c　uǒ → cuǒ　　　dǐ → d　ǐ → dǐ
cuò → c　uò → cuò　　　dì → d　ì → dì

tōng → t ōng → tōng
tóng → t óng → tóng
tǒng → t ǒng → tǒng
tòng → t òng → tòng

méi → m éi → méi
měi → m ěi → měi
mèi → m èi → mèi

二、听录音并熟读下面的句子。

Listen to the recording and read the following sentences till you learn them by heart.

1. Bú cuò a!
不 错 啊!

2. Qǐng kè a!
请 客 啊!

3. Huàmiàn hěn měi.
画面 很 美。

4. Shēngyīn yě bú cuò.
声音 也 不 错。

三、跟读并辨别下面音节。

Read the following syllables and try to tell one from the other.

nǎli—nàli
guòjiǎng—guòjiàng
búcuò—búzuò
qǐngkè—jīngguò

四、请让我们一起再学习几个常用的词语，然后做练习。

Learn more useful words before you do the exercises.

补充词语 Supplementary Words

能干	nénggàn	（形）	capable	*(adj.)*
棒	bàng	（形）	good	*(adj.)*

选择填空 Fill in the Blanks with Appropriate Words

guòjiǎng(过奖)　　xíng(行)　　zhēn(真)

1. A：Xiǎo Lǐ，nǐ zhēn nénggàn!
   A：小 李，你 真 能干!
   B：＿＿＿＿＿＿＿＿ 了。

2. A：Nǐ zhēn
   A：你 真＿＿＿＿＿＿＿!
   B：Nǐ guòjiǎng le.
   B：你 过奖 了。

3. A：Nǐ　　　　　xíng!
   A：你＿＿＿＿＿＿＿行!
   B：Nín guòjiǎng le.
   B：您 过奖 了。

4. A：Lǐ Lín，nǐ zhēn bàng!
   A：李 琳，你 真 棒!
   B：　　　　　　le
   B：＿＿＿＿＿＿＿＿ 了。

五、请你仔细体会下面的句子中“行”的意思有什么不同。

Figure out the meaning of “xíng” in the following sentences.

1. Xíng，wǒ lái.
   行，我 来。

2. Bù xíng a，wǒ bù néng qù.
   不 行 啊，我 不 能 去。

3. Nǐ zhēn xíng!
   你 真 行!

六、把下面表达相同意思的汉字、拼音、英文用线连起来。

Connect the equivalent sentences in *pinyin*, characters and English in the three columns with a line.

A.你真行！	1.Shēngyīn yě bú cuò.	(1) The picture is really beautiful.
B.画面很美。	2.Nǐ zhēn xíng!	(2) Its sound effect is pleasant
C.声音也不错。	3.Huàmiàn hěn měi.	(3) You are really terrific!

七、下面的情景用汉语你知道该怎么说吗？请试一试。

Try to express yourself in the following situations.

1.你的同事有了新发明，你对他表示称赞。
Pay a compliment to your colleague on his new inventions.

2.你的朋友做了一桌好菜，你边品尝边赞赏。
Express your appreciation of the good dishes your friend has prepared for you.

3.你的孩子得了奖状，你对孩子说什么？
How will you praise your child for the certificate of merit he has been awarded?

八、汉字点击。

Open the CD to view the characters.

请通过光盘点击认读、书写下面的汉字。请注意汉字书写时的笔顺。

Open the CD, click the buttons, read and write the following characters, paying attention to their stroke-order.

错　得　同　事　行　画　面　美　声　音　喜　欢

自我评估 Self-assessment

1.你对自己的进度满意吗？
Are you satisfied about about your progress in learning Chinese?

2.中国人说话你现在能听懂多少了?

How well can you follow a native Chinese speaker?

3.你现在能跟中国人用中国话交际了吗?

Are you able to use Chinese in your communication with Chinese people?

文化点击 Cultural Points

中国人的谦虚　Chinese Modesty

中华民族是一个自谦的民族，不喜欢炫耀自己的优势，而对自己的成绩却常常低调处理。在得到褒奖时，一般总是谦虚地说自己还有很多不足，做得还很不够等等。所以当你听到中国人对你的夸奖表示“哪里，哪里”时，你千万不要以为他们不同意你的夸奖，尽管他们心里非常高兴，但还是要客气一下，以示谦虚。否则就会被当做自高自大的人。

现代中国的一部分人，特别是年轻人、“文化人”，他们在跟外国人交往中，已经“洋化”了，也常常用“谢谢”来回答夸奖。

Traditionally the Chinese people do not to like to show a high opinion of their own merits. Instead they are always modest about their achievements, or prefer a low-key statement to a display of their advantages. When you praised a Chinese person, he may humbly tell you how deficient he is. Therefore the Chinese reply “nǎli, nǎli” (well, it is nothing) to any complimentary remarks may not be interpreted as a denial of the truth. However grateful they are they may not verbalize their thanks, or they will be considered to be insufferable people.

Nowadays some people, especially young and educated Chinese, like to follow the English way and thank admirers for their compliments.

Dì-shísì kè Zàijiàn
第 14 课 再见
Lesson 14 Good-bye

导学 Guiding Remarks

当你和朋友告别时，一定是要说道别的话的。本课将教给你最常用的几句话。

You say all your good-byes when you take leave of your friends. In this lesson you are going to learn a few useful Chinese expressions for bidding farewell.

A

John is saying good-bye to Mike before he leaves for the United States of America.

Màikē: Zhè jiù zǒu ma?
麦克：这 就 走 吗？
Mike: Are you leaving right now?

John: Duì.
John: 对。I've booked my ticket.
John: Yes, I am.

Màikē: Huānyíng nǐ zài lái!
麦克：欢迎　你 再 来！
Mike: Come again, and a warm welcome awaits you.

John: Xièxie!
John: 谢谢！
John: Thank you!

Màikē: Xīwàng wǒmen zǎorì zài jiàn miàn?
麦克：希望　我们 早日 再 见 面。
Mike: I hope it won't be long before we meet again.

John: Wǒ yě shì. Zàijiàn!
John: 我 也 是。再见！
John: So do I. Good-bye!

Màikē: Zàijiàn!
麦克：再见！
Mike: Good-bye!

John: Zàijiàn!
John: 再见！
John: Good-bye!

B

John says good-bye to all staff members in the office.

John：Wǒ yào zǒu le.
John：我 要 走了。
John：I am leaving.

Wáng Guāng：Wǒmen huì xiǎng nǐ de.
王 光：我们 会 想 你的。
Wang Guang：We'll miss you.

John：Xièxie! Wǒ yě huì xiǎng nǐmen de.
John：谢谢！我 也 会 想 你们 的。
John：How nice of you. I will miss you too.

Wáng Guāng：Huānyíng nǐ zài lái!
王 光：欢迎 你 再 来！
Wang Guang：Hope you'll come here for a second visit.

John：Xièxie! Zàijiàn!
John：谢谢！ 再见！
John：Thank you for your hospitality! Good-bye!

Wáng Guāng：Zàijiàn!
王 光：再见！
Wang Guang：Good-bye!

词 语 Word List

1.再见	zàijiàn	(动)	good-bye	(v.)
2.就	jiù	(副)	right now	(adv.)
3.对	duì	(形)	correct	(adj.)
4.再	zài	(副)	again	(adv.)
5.希望	xīwàng	(动)	to hope	(v.)
6.早日	zǎorì	(副)	soon	(adv.)
7.见面	jiàn miàn		to see, to meet	
8.要	yào	(动)	to be going to	(v.)
9.会	huì	(动)	will	(v.)
10.想	xiǎng	(动)	to miss	(v.)

语言点链接 Language Points

"要……了" The Usage of "yào...le"

"要……了"是表示马上去做某事或表示某种动作或行为即将发生。如"我要走了"是"我马上就走了","我们要见面了"指的是"我们马上就能见面了"。

"yào...le" is often used to indicate that something (or some act) is going to take place, as in "wǒ yào zǒu le"(I am leaving) and "wǒmen yào jiàn miàn le"(We'll meet soon).

练 习 Exercises

一、请听录音或跟着老师读。

Listen to the recording or read after the teacher.

jiū → j iū → jiū	zōu → z ōu → zōu
jiǔ → j iǔ → jiǔ	zǒu → z ǒu → zǒu
jiù → j iù → jiù	zòu → z òu → zòu

duī → d uī → duī
duì → d uì → duì

zāo → z āo → zāo
záo → z áo → záo
zǎo → z ǎo → zǎo
zào → z ào → zào

mián → m ián → mián
miǎn → m iǎn → miǎn
miàn → m iàn → miàn

xiāng → x iāng → xiāng
xiáng → x iáng → xiáng
xiǎng → x iǎng → xiǎng
xiàng → x iàng → xiàng

xī → x ī → xī
xí → x í → xí
xǐ → x ǐ → xǐ
xì → x ì → xì

rì → r ì → rì

huī → h uī → huī
huí → h uí → huí
huǐ → h uǐ → huǐ
huì → h uì → huì

二、听录音并熟读下面的句子。

Read the following sentences till you learn them by heart.

1. Zhè jiù zǒu ma?
   这 就 走 吗?

2. Huānyíng nǐ zài lái.
   欢迎 你 再 来。

3. Xīwàng wǒmen zǎorì zài jiàn miàn.
   希望 我们 早日 再 见 面。

4. Wǒ yào zǒu le.
   我 要 走 了。

5. Wǒmen huì xiǎng nǐ de.
   我们 会 想 你 的。

6. Zàijiàn!
   再见!

三、跟读并辨别下面音节。

Read the following syllables and try to tell one from the other.

zàijiàn—cáijiǎn
jiànmiàn—qiánmiàn
xīwàng—qīwàng
cǎodì—zǎorì

四、请让我们一起再学习几个常用的词语，然后做练习。

Learn more useful words before you do the exercises.

补充词语　Supplementary Words

回	huí	（动）	to return	*(v.)*
国	guó	（名）	country	*(n.)*
分别	fēnbié	（动）	to say good-bye, to separate	*(v.)*

选择填空　Fill in the Blanks with Appropriate Words

zàijiàn (再见)　　　　zài lái (再来)

1. A: Xiǎo Lǐ, wǒ yào huí guó le, zàijiàn!
   A: 小　李，我　要　回　国了，再见!
   B: ______________________!

2. A: Wǒmen yào fēnbié le, zàijiàn!
   A: 我们　　要　分别　了，　再见!
   B: ______________________!

3. A: Xiǎo Wáng, huānyíng nǐ
   A: 小　　王，　　欢迎　你 __________。
   B: Xièxie!
   B: 谢谢!

4. A: Xiǎo Wáng, zàijiàn!
   A: 小　　王，　再见!
   B: ______________________!

五、试着把下面的词语加上汉语拼音。

Transliterate the following characters into *pinyin*.

再见　　欢迎　　市场　　经理　　秘书

六、把下面表达相同意思的汉字、拼音、英文用线连起来。

Connect the equivalent sentences in *pinyin*, characters and English in the three columns with a line.

A. 这就走吗?	Huānyíng nǐ zài lái.	(1) You are welcome to come again
B. 我要走了。	Zhè jiù zǒu ma?	(2) I am leaving.
C. 欢迎你再来。	Wǒ yào zǒu le.	(3) Are you leaving right now?

七、下面的情景用汉语你知道该怎么说吗?请试一试。

Express yourself in the following situations.

1. 你的同事要回国了,临别时你用汉语向他告别。
   How will you say good-bye in Chinese to your colleague who is leaving for his hometown?

2. 朋友到你家里做客,告别时你对他说什么?
   What will you say to your friend who is leaving after a visit to your place.

3. 你送你的家人去外地旅游,在车站你用汉语跟他们告别。
   How will you say good-bye in Chinese to your family at the railway station when they are about to start on a journey?

八、汉字点击。

Open the CD to view the characters.

请通过光盘点击认读、书写下面的汉字。请注意汉字书写时的笔顺。

Open the CD, click the buttons, read and write the following characters, paying attention to their stroke-order.

就　走　对　再　希　望　早　日　会　想

自我评估 Self-assessment

1.你认为汉语的道别语复杂吗？

Do you think the Chinese expressions for farewell are complicated to learn?

2.通过这段时间的学习，你对中国的语言和文化了解了多少？

What progress have you made in learning the Chinese language and culture?

3.现在你的进度是不是更快了？

Do you find that you are able to learn the lessons much faster than before?

文化点击 Cultural Points

送行　Seeing People Off

中国是一个热情好客的民族，客人告辞时，主人一般都要送一送。送得越远越表示热情和礼貌，一般至少也要送出自己的家门或办公室门外，并且要目送客人走远，直到看不见为止。有时要送到很远，比如一直送到客人上车，再目送车开走。切记不能客人一出去，马上转身关门。

Chinese people are justly famous for their hospitality. A Chinese host often personally accompanies the leaving guests to the lift, or goes with them until they are out of his house or office, or even stands gazing after their parting. The farther the host escorts the guests, the greater an honour it will be. A good send-off is commonly given to the guests until they get into the car. It is unusual to immediately shut the door behind guests.

Dì-shíwǔkè　Zhù nǐ yílù píng'ān
第 15 课　祝你一路平安
Lesson 15　Have a Pleasant Journey

导学 Guiding Remarks

送朋友离别时，你要说几句祝福的话。下面就是中国人对远行者的祝福。记住了会很有用的。

Good wishes are always given to friends when parting. In the following dialogues you will learn about Chinese expressions of good wishes to those going on a long journey. Learn them by heart and they will turn out to be useful some day.

课文 Text

A

John's colleagues come out to give him a warm send-off.

John：Zàijiàn!
John：再见!
John：Good-bye!

Wáng Guāng：Wǒmen sòngsong nǐ.
王 光：我们 送送 你。
Wang Guang：Let's walk with you.

John：Bú yòng le. Qǐng liú bù.
John：不 用 了。请 留 步。
John：Don't bother to come any further.

Wáng Guāng：Zhù nǐ lǚtú yúkuài!
王 光：祝 你旅途 愉快!
Wang Guang：Wish you a pleasant journey!

John：Xièxie!
John：谢谢!
John：Thank you!

Wáng Guāng：Zàijiàn!
王 光：再见!
Wang Guang：Good-bye!

John：Zàijiàn!
John：再见!
John：Good-bye, everybody!

B

Li Lin accompanies John till he gets into the car.

John：Xièxie nǐ de zhàogu.
John：谢谢 你 的 照顾。
John：Thank you for the trouble you've taken on my behalf during my stay in China.

Lǐ Lín：Nǎli, nǎli. Nǐ tài kèqi le.
李 琳：哪里，哪里。你 太 客气 了。
Li Lin：Well, that's nothing really. It's very kind of you to say so.

John：Wǒ zǒu le.
John：(Getting into the car)我 走 了。
John：Now I am going.

Lǐ Lín：Hǎo, huānyíng zài lái.
李 琳：(Handshaking with John) 好， 欢迎 再 来。
Li Lin：Take care. Looking forward to your second visit.

John：Xièxie!
John：谢谢!
John：Thank you!

Lǐ Lín：Zhù nǐ yílù píng'ān!
李 琳：祝 你 一路 平安!
Li Lin：Have a pleasant journey!

John：Xièxie! Zàijiàn!
John：谢谢。再见!
John：Thank you. Good-bye!

Lǐ Lín：Zàijiàn!
李 琳：再见!
Li Lin：Good-bye!

词　语　Word List

1.祝	zhù	(动)	to wish	*(v.)*
2.一路	yílù	(名)	all the way	*(n.)*
3.平安	píng'ān	(形)	safe	*(adj.)*
4.送	sòng	(动)	to see off	*(v.)*
5.留步	liú bù	(动)	don't bother to come any further	*(v.)*
6.旅途	lǚtú	(名)	trip	*(n.)*
7.愉快	yúkuài	(形)	pleasant	*(adj.)*
8.照顾	zhàogu	(动)	to take care of	*(v.)*
9.哪里	nǎli	(代)	not at all, where	*(pron.)*
10.太	tài	(副)	too	*(adv.)*

语言点链接　Language Points

省略句 Elliptical Sentences

在说话双方都明确意思的情况下，汉语常常用一种最简明的方式来表达，省略其中的一些成分，因而称为省略句。省略句有的可以补出省略的成分，如第5课中的"见到你很高兴"就是省略了"我"。在这句中，如果要补充完整，"我"可以放在句首，即"我见到你很高兴"；也可以放在句中，即"见到你我很高兴"。第9课中的"资料呢？"指的是"资料在哪里？"省略了后面部分。还有的省略句不需要或不可能补出省略的成分，如第9课中的"对不起"、"没关系"，第10课中的"可以"就不能补出，但一点也不影响表达。

A Chinese elliptical sentence is a simple statement in which some missing constituents are understood by both the speaker and listener. Some of the omitted constituents may be restored. For example, the elliptical sentence"jiàndào nǐ hěn gāoxìng"(Lesson 5) with the missing word "wǒ" is derived from "wǒ jiàndào nǐ hěn gāoxìng" or "jiàndào nǐ wǒ hěn gāoxìng". Similarly the phrase "zīliào ne"(lesson 9) is derived from "zīliào zài nǎli ne". Some of the missing constituents may not be or are unnecessarily restored as in "duì buqǐ","méiguānxi" (lesson 9) and "kěyǐ" (lesson 10), but nobody worries about being misunderstood.

练 习 Exercises

一、请听录音或跟着老师读。

Listen to the recording or read after the teacher.

sōng → s ōng → sōng
sóng → s óng → sóng
sǒng → s ǒng → sǒng
sòng → s òng → sòng

lǘ → l ǘ → lǘ
lǚ → l ǚ → lǚ
lǜ → l ǜ → lǜ

shū → sh ū → shū
shú → sh ú → shú
shǔ → sh ǔ → shǔ
shù → sh ù → shù

zhāo → zh āo → zhāo
zháo → zh áo → zháo
zhǎo → zh ǎo → zhǎo
zhào → zh ào → zhào

tāi → t āi → tāi
tái → t ái → tái
tǎi → t ǎi → tǎi
tài → t ài → tài

pīng → p īng → pīng
píng → p íng → píng

zhū → zh ū → zhū
zhú → zh ú → zhú
zhǔ → zh ǔ → zhǔ
zhù → zh ù → zhù

tū → t ū → tū
tú → t ú → tú
tǔ → t ǔ → tǔ
tù → t ù → tù

gū → g ū → gū
gǔ → g ǔ → gǔ
gù → g ù → gù

lū → l ū → lū
lú → l ú → lú
lǔ → l ǔ → lǔ
lù → l ù → lù

yū → y ū → yū
yú → y ú → yú
yǔ → y ǔ → yǔ
yù → y ù → yù

二、听录音并熟读下面的句子。

Listen to the recording, read the following sentences till you learn them by heart.

1. Wǒmen sòngsong nǐ.
   我们　送送　你。

2. Qǐng liú bù.
   请　留步。

3. Zhù nǐ lǚtú yúkuài!
   祝　你　旅途　愉快！

4. Nǐ tài kèqi le.
   你　太　客气了。

5. Xièxie nǐ de zhàogu.
   谢谢　你　的　照顾。

6. Zhù nǐ yílù píng'ān!
   祝　你　一路　平安！

三、跟读并辨别下面音节。

Read the following syllables after the teacher and try to tell one from the other.

yílù—yílǜ
píng'ān—pínjiàn
zhàogu—sàozhou
shènglì—shùnlì

四、请让我们一起再学习几个常用的词语，然后做练习。

Learn more useful words before you do the exercises.

补充词语 Supplementary Words

顺风	shùnfēng	（动）	to have a favourable wind	(v.)
保重	bǎozhòng	（动）	to take care	(v.)

选择填空 Fill in the Blanks with Appropriate Words

píng'ān(平安)　yílù(一路)　zàijiàn(再见)　zhù(祝)

1. A: Xiǎo Lǐ, yílù duō bǎozhòng! Zàijiàn!
   A: 小　李，一路 多　保重！　再见！
   B: ______________________!

2. A: Zhù nǐ 　　　　　　　shùnfēng!
   A: 祝　你 ______________ 顺风！
   B: Xièxie!
   B: 谢谢！

3. A: Xiǎo Wáng, 　　　　nǐ lǚtú yúkuài!
   A: 小　王，_______ 你 旅途 愉快！
   B: Xièxie! Zàijiàn!
   B: 谢谢！　再见！

4. A: Zhù nǐ　yílù
   A: 祝　你 一路 _____________!
   B: Zàijiàn!
   B: 再见！

五、请把下面的句子加上汉语拼音。

Transliterate the following sentences into *pinyin*.

1. 祝你旅途顺利！

2. 我们会想你的。

3. 谢谢你的帮忙。

六、把下面表达相同意思的汉字、拼音、英文用线连起来。

Connect the equivalent sentences in *pinyin*, characters and English in the three columns with a line.

A. 请留步。	1. Qǐng liú bù.	(1) Have a good journey!
B. 你太客气了。	2. Zhùn nǐ yílù píng'ān!	(2) Don't bother to come any further.
C. 祝你一路平安!	3. Nǐ tài kèqi le.	(3) It's very kind of you!

七、下面的情景用汉语你知道该怎么说吗？请试一试。

Try to express yourself in the following situations.

1. 你在车站和你的朋友道别，请用汉语祝福他旅途平安。
   Say "have a pleasant journey" in Chinese to your friend who is leaving by train.

2. 朋友要回国了，他临走前你对他说祝福的话。
   Wish a good journey to your friend who is leaving for home.

3. 你送同事去出差，临别用汉语表达祝福。
   Express good wishes in Chinese to your colleague who is on a business trip.

八、汉字点击。

Open the CD to view the characters.

请通过光盘点击认读、书写下面的汉字。请注意汉字书写时的笔顺。

Open the CD, click the buttons, read and write the following Chinese characters, focusing your attention on their stroke-order.

送　留　步　祝　旅　途　愉　快　照　顾　太　路　平　安

自我评估 Self-assessment

1. 现在你为朋友送行时知道说什么了吧?
   Do you know the Chinese expressions that are applicable to a send-off?

2. 你的中国朋友在为你送别时还说过什么话?
   What did your Chinese friends say to you when they saw you off?

3.你最喜欢中国人对你说什么？
What are the Chinese expressions you prefer at parting?

文化点击 Cultural Points

中国人的祝福 Chinese expressions of good wishes

在送行时，在节日里，在过生日的时候，人们都喜欢说一些祝福的话。中国人在不同的场景用不同的话来表达，而且很丰富。比如，在生日里有："生日快乐！""祝你健康长寿！""祝您福如东海，寿比南山！"等；送行时有："一路平安！""一路顺利！""旅途愉快！""一路顺风！"等；过新年时更有很多吉祥祝福的话，如："新年快乐！""新年吉祥！""新年好！""合家幸福！"等等。

Chinese good wishes are expressed on holidays and festivals, or at birthday parties. Such expressions vary from one to another. The most commonly used ones are "shērì kuàilè"(Happy birthday), "zhù nǐ jiànkāng chángshòu" (Wish you good health and long life), "zhù nǐ fú rú Dōnghǎi, shòubǐ Nánshān" (May your happiness be as boundless as the sea and longevity comparable to that of the hills), "yílù píng'ān"(Bon voyage), "yílù shùnlì"(Have a good trip), "lǚtú yúkuài"(Have a peasant journey), "yílù shùnfēng"(Have a plain sailing), " xīnnián kuàilè"(Happy New Year), "xīnnián jíxiáng"(Have an auspicious New Year), "xīnnián hǎo"(Happy New Year), and "héjiā xìngfú"(Wish your family every happiness).

Dì-shíliù kè　Dǎrǎo yíxià
第 16 课　打扰 一下
Lesson 16　Sorry to Trouble You a Moment

导学 Guiding Remarks

当你有事要影响对方或要打扰对方时，你应该说一句表示客气的话，这样才能得到别人的谅解，别人也愿意为你提供方便。本课就教你几句表达抱歉的话。

A request should be made before one breaks the quiet or order of others, so that one gets the permission and avoid their hard feelings toward any inconvenience. In this lesson we will deal with some useful sentences for this purpose.

课文 Text

A

Li Lin comes in when Mike is reading documents.

Lǐ lín: Duìbuqǐ, dǎrǎo yíxià.
李琳：对不起，　打扰　一下。
Li Lin: Excuse me, can I disturb you for a while?

Màikè: Shénme shì?
麦克：什么　　事？
Mike: What can I do for you?

Lǐ Lín: Zhèi wèi kèhù jīntiān kěyǐ jiàn ma?
李琳：这　位 客户　今天　可以 见　吗？
Li Lin: Are you going to meet the customer today?

Mike wants to check the work schedule in a file, but it's on the other side of the table. Pointing his finger to it, he asks Li to get it for him.

Màikè: Máfan nǐ dì gěi wǒ.
麦克：麻烦　你 递 给　我。
Mike: Will you pass me the file?

Li Lin passes it to him. He checks the arrangement for the day.

Màikè: Kěyǐ jiàn.
麦克：可以　见。
Mike: Yes, I am.

B

After a meeting the employees are walking along the corridor. Wang Guang catches up with Li Lin who is chatting with her colleague.

Wáng Guāng：Lǐ Lín, duìbuqǐ, dǎrǎo yíxià.
王 光：李 琳，对不起，　打扰 一下。(apologetically nodding to her colleague.)
Wang Guang：Sorry to interrupt, Li Lin.

Lǐ Lín：Shénme shì?
李 琳：什么　事？
Li Lin：Can I help you?

Wáng Guāng：Máfan nǐ jiāo gěi Màizǒng.
王 光：麻烦 你 交 给　麦总。(handing her something.)
Wang Guang：Will you please pass it on to Maizong?

Lǐ Lín：Zhè shì shénme?
李 琳：(Puzzling over it)这　是　什么？
Li Lin：What's it?

Wáng Guāng：Wǒ de bàogào ā.
王 光：我 的 报告 啊。
Wang Guang：That's my report.

Li Lin returns Wang the paper. He opens it. To his surprise it is nothing but a blank sheet of paper.

Wáng Guāng: Á? Duìbuqǐ, qǐng ná yíxià.
王光：啊？对不起，请拿一下。
Wang Guang: What? Sorry, but keep it for the time being.

Wang leaves it in her hand and returns to the meeting room where his report was found lying on the floor. Hurriedly he comes back with it.

Wáng Guāng: Duìbuqǐ, zài zhèr.
王光：对不起，在这儿。
Wang Guang: That's my fault. Here it is.

Lǐ Lín: Hǎo, wǒ yídìng jiāo gěi Màizǒng.
李琳：(Looking at it)好，我一定交给麦总。
Li Lin: Don't worry, I'll submit it to Maizong for you.

Wáng Guāng: Xièxie!
王光：谢谢！
Wang Guang: Thank you!

词语 Word List

1.打扰	dǎrǎo	(动)	to disturb, to bother	(v.)
2.什么	shénme	(代)	what	(pron.)
3.事	shì	(名)	thing, matter	(n.)
4.今天	jīntiān	(名)	today	(n.)
5.麻烦	máfan	(动)	to trouble	(v.)
6.递	dì	(动)	to pass on to	(v.)
7.交	jiāo	(动)	to hand, to submit	(v.)
8.报告	bàogào	(名)	report	(n.)
9.拿	ná	(动)	to take	(v.)
10.一定	yídìng	(副)	surely	(adv.)

语言点链接 Language Points

动量词　Verbal Measure Words

汉语中表示动作次数的词语叫动量词。动量词位置在动词的后面，说明动作的次数。动量词的选用和动词有关系，也和动作的对象有关系，有时一个动词有几个可以使用的动量词。下面是本册中常用的动词和动量词的搭配表（以"一"为数词）。

Verbal measure words are used after a verb to indicate the frequency of an action. The choice of verbal measure words is decided by the specific verb and the target the action is taken toward. There may be a couple of measure words that are applicable to the same verb. The following is a table of collocation of Chinese verbs and their corresponding measure words (with "yī" as the basic numeral in the given phrases).

动词	拼音	动量词	拼音	英译
打	dǎ	一下	yí xià	Beat
来	lái	一次／趟	yí cì/tàng	Come
走	zǒu	一步	yí bù	Walk
说	shuō	一句	yí jù	Say
问	wèn	一声／句	yì shēng/yí jù	Ask
买	mǎi	一次／回	yí cì/yì huí	Buy
去	qù	一趟／次	yí tàng /cì	Go
看	kàn	一下（手表） 一回（电影）	yí xià (shǒubiǎo) yì huí (diànyǐng)	Have a look at (a watch); see a film
写	xiě	一手／笔（好字）	yì shǒu/bǐ (hǎozì)	Write beautifully
拿	ná	一下（笔）	yí xià (bǐ)	Take (a pen)
签	qiān	一下（字）	yí xià (zì)	Sign (one's name)
请	qǐng	一次（客）	yí cì (kè)	Invite
给	gěi	一次（机会）	yí cì (jīhuì)	Have a chance
见	jiàn	一次（面）	yí cì (miàn)	Meet
进	jìn	一次（城）	yí cì (chéng)	Go into (town)
送	sòng	一回（礼）	yì huí (lǐ)	Present (a gift)
谈	tán	一次（话）	yí cì (huà)	Have (a chat)
用	yòng	一次（电脑）	yí cì (diànniǎo)	Use (a computer)

练 习 Exercises

一、请听录音或跟着老师读。

Listen to the recording or read after the teacher.

ráo → r áo → ráo
rǎo → r ǎo → rǎo
rào → r ào → rào

shēn → sh ēn → shēn
shén → sh én → shén
shěn → sh ěn → shěn
shèn → sh èn → shèn

tiān → t iān → tiān
tián → t ián → tián
tiǎn → t iǎn → tiǎn
tiàn → t iàn → tiàn

fān → f ān → fān
fán → f án → fán
fǎn → f ǎn → fǎn
fàn → f àn → fàn

dī → d ī → dī
dí → d í → dí
dǐ → d ǐ → dǐ
dì → d ì → dì

bāo → b āo → bāo
báo → b áo → báo
bǎo → b ǎo → bǎo
bào → bào → bào

dīng → d īng → dīng
dǐng → d ǐng → dǐng
dìng → d ìng → dìng

zhuān→zh uān→zhuān
zhuǎn→zh uǎn→zhuǎn
zhuàn→zh uàn→zhuàn

二、听录音并熟读下面的句子。

Listen to the recording and read the following sentences till you learn them by heart.

1. Duìbuqǐ, dǎrǎo yíxià.
对不起， 打扰 一下。

2. Shénme shì?
什么 事？

3. Zhèi wèi kèhù jīntiān kěyǐ jiàn ma?
这 位 客户 今天 可以 见 吗？

4. Máfan nǐ dǐ gěi wǒ.
麻烦 你 递 给 我。

5. Máfan nǐ jiāo gěi Màizǒng.
麻烦 你 交 给 麦总。

6. Wǒ yídìng jiāo gěi Màizǒng.
我 一定 交 给 麦总。

三、跟读并辨别下面音节。

Read the following syllables and try to tell one from the other.

máfan–yāhuán
jīntiān–jīngyàn
yídìng–yídòng
dǎrǎo–dàjiào

四、请让我们一起再学习几个常用的词语，然后做练习。

Learn more useful words before you do the exercises.

补充词语 Supplementary Words

过	guò	（动）	to go through	*(v.)*
过去	guòqu	（动）	to pass	*(v.)*

选择填空 Fill in the Blanks with Appropriate Words

qǐng(请) guò(过) bú kèqi(不客气) xiān(先)

1. A：Bàoqiàn，dǎrǎo yíxià, xièxie!
A：抱歉， 打扰 一下，谢谢！
B：________________________！

2. A：Máfan nǐ yíxià, wǒ xiān qù. Xièxie!
A：麻烦 你 一下，我 先__________去。谢谢！
B：Bú yòng xiè.
B：不 用 谢。

3.A： nǐ jiāo gěi Màizǒng hǎo ma?
A：________你 交 给 麦总 好 吗？
B：Kěyǐ.
B：可以。

4.A：Dǎrǎo yíxià, wǒ ________ guòqu.
A：打扰 一下，我________过去。
B：Hǎo ba.
B：好 吧。

五、请试着给下面的词语加上拼音，并在右边的英文解释中找出相对的意思

Transliterate the following words into *pinyin* and match them with appropriate English definitions given on the right.

打扰	to pass on
转交	to trouble
麻烦	to disturb

六、把下面表达相同意思的汉字、拼音、英文用线连起来。

Connect the equivalent sentences in *pinyin*, characters and English in the three columns with a line.

A.打扰一下。	1.Dǎrǎo yíxià.	(1) What can I do for you?
B.我一定转交。	2.Shénme shì?	(2) May I trouble you...
C.什么事？	3.Wǒ yídìng zhuǎn jiāo.	(3) I'll pass it on to...

七、下面的情景用汉语你知道该怎么说吗？请试一试。

Try to express yourself in the following situations.

1. 你有急事需要先上车，请用汉语对旁边的人表示歉意。
   What would you say in Chinese if you wanted to get into a car before other people?

2. 你的朋友正在说话，你要打断他一下，请用汉语对他先表达抱歉的意思。
   What's the Chinese for "sorry to interrupt" for breaking your friends' talking?

3. 你想问路，在路上看到两个人正在谈话，你在问路前要先对他们说什么？
   What would you say in Chinese before you ask the way to two people who are chatting?

八、汉字点击。

Open the CD to view the characters.

请通过光盘点击认读、书写下面的汉字。请注意汉字书写时的笔顺。

Open the CD, read and write the following characters with special attention to their stroke-order.

打 扰 什 今 天 麻 烦 递 交 报 告 拿 定 转

自我评估 Self-assessment

1. 现在当你遇到了困难时，可以用汉语请求别人帮忙吗？
   Do you know how to ask for help in Chinese?

2. 你对自己的进度满意吗？
   Are you happy about your progress in learning Chinese?

3. 你的汉字写得怎么样？
   How well can you write Chinese characters?

文化点击 Cultural Points

中国人的理财观念 How do the Chinese manage their money matters

传统的中国人一般在花钱时都要精打细算、量入为出，讲究有多少钱，办多大事。大多数人都要努力存点钱，这样心里才踏实，而不喜欢把手中的钱全部花光。所以他们在消费上都要以首先有了钱为前提，即使是手中持有信用卡的人，也不喜欢透支。

Traditionally the average Chinese are careful with their budgeting. Instead of spending more than their monthly income, they try to keep their daily expenditures by depositing the unused money in a bank. Therefore purchases are often made when usable cash is on hand. Credit card holders, by and large, consider it unwise to call upon a bank account overdraft.

Dì-shíqī kè　Nǐ hǎo ma
第 17 课　你好吗
Lesson 17　How Are You

导学 Guiding Remarks

在老朋友见面或打电话时，我们常常要寒暄一下以示关心。汉语中表示寒暄的话有很多，先学会这几句，会帮助你解决问题的。

When we meet our old friends or begin a telephone conversation, we often exchange amenities with one another. There are many courteous Chinese expressions of which some will be dealt with in the lesson. Surely you will find them useful in your daily communication with Chinese people.

A

Mike is making a phone call.

John：Màikē，nǐ hǎo!
John：麦克，你 好!
John：Hello，Mike!

Màikē：Shì nǐ a，John. Nǐ hǎo ma?
麦克：是 你 啊，John。你 好 吗?
Mike：Oh，it's you，John. How are you?

John：Wǒ hěn hǎo，nǐ ne?
John：我 很 好，你 呢?
John：I am fine，and you?

Màikē：Wǒ yě hěn hǎo.
麦克：我 也 很 好。
Mike：Very well，thank you.

John：Máng ma?
John：忙 吗?
John：Are you busy these days?

Màikē：Hěn máng.
麦克：很 忙。
Mike：Yes，we are.

John：Shēntǐ hǎo ma?
John：身体 好 吗?
John：How are you keeping?

Màikē：Hái hǎo.
麦克：还 好。
Mike：Quite well.

John：Wǒ xià gè xīngqī qù Zhōngguó.
John：我 下 个 星期 去 中国。
John：I am going to China next week.

Màikè：Shì ma? Tài hǎo le!
麦克：是 吗？太 好 了！
Mike：Are you? That's great!

B

Wang Guang is talking with a customer.

Wáng Guāng：Nǐ hǎo!
王 光：你 好！
Wang Guang：Good Morning!

Kèhù：Nǐ hǎo!
客户：你 好！
Customer：Good Morning!

Wáng Guāng：Hǎo jiǔ bú jiàn, nǐ hǎo ba?
王 光：好 久不 见，你 好 吧？
Wang Guang：Haven't seen you for ages. How are you?

Kèhù：Hái hǎo. Nǐ máng ma?
客户：还 好。你 忙 吗？
Customer：Not bad, so to say. Very much involved in your work?

Wáng Guāng：Hěn máng. Nǐ ne?
王 光：很 忙。你 呢？
Wang Guang：Yes, I am. What about you?

Kèhù：Wǒ yě hěn máng.
客户：我 也 很 忙。
Customer：So am I.

Wáng Guāng：Shēngyì zěnmeyàng?
王 光：生意 怎么样？
Wang Guang：How is your business?

Kèhù：Mǎmǎhūhū.
客户：马马虎虎。
Customer：Just so so, I am afraid.

词语 Word List

1.忙	máng	（形）	busy	*(adj.)*
2.身体	Shēntǐ	（名）	health	*(n.)*
3.还	hái	（副）	also	*(adv.)*
4.下	xià	（名）	next	*(n.)*
5.星期	xīngqī	（名）	week	*(n.)*
6.去	qù	（动）	to go	*(v.)*
7.中国	Zhōngguó	（专名）	China	*(pn.)*
8.好久	hǎo jiǔ	（名）	long time	*(n.)*
9.生意	shēngyì	（名）	business	*(n.)*
10.怎么样	zěnmeyàng	（代）	How	*(pron.)*
11.马马虎虎	mǎmǎhūhū	（形）	just so so	*(adj.)*

语言点链接 Language Points

1.“啊”的语流音变 Contextual Sound Change of “a”

“啊”在句子末尾时，常常因为受到它前面的音节末尾音素的影响而发生音变。规律是：

（1）前面的音素是 i、ü 时读 ya。

（2）前面的音素是 u(包括 ao/iao)时读做 wa。

（3）前面的音素是 n 时读做 na。

The pronunciation of the modal particle “a” changes when preceded by the different end of a syllable.

(1) It becomes “ya” when preceded by “i”,“ü”.

(2) It becomes “wa” when preceded by “u”(“ao” and “iao” included).

(3) It becomes “na” when preceded by “n”.

2.一个星期中的七天 Seven Days in a Week

汉 字	拼 音	英 译
星期一	xīngqīyī	Monday
星期二	xīngqī'èr	Tuesday
星期三	xīngqīsān	Wednesday

星期四	xīngqīsì	Thursday
星期五	xīngqīwǔ	Friday
星期六	xīngqīliù	Saturday
星期日	xīngqīrì	Sunday

练 习 Exercises

一、请听录音或跟着老师读。

Listen to the recording or read after the teacher.

māng → m āng → māng
máng → m áng → máng
mǎng → m ǎng → mǎng

xiā → x iā → xiā
xiá → x iá → xiá
xià → xià → xià

qū → q ū → qū
qú → q ú → qú
qǔ → q ǔ → qǔ
qù → q ù → qù

zhōng → zh ōng → zhōng
zhōng → zh ǒng → zhǒng
zhòng → zh òng → zhòng

tī → t ī → tī
tí → t í → tí
tǐ → t ǐ → tǐ
tì → t ì → tì

guō → g uō → guō
guó → g uó → guó
guǒ → g uǒ → guǒ
guò → g uò → guò

yāng → y āng → yāng
yáng → y áng → yáng
yǎng → y ǎng → yǎng
yàng → y àng → yàng

shēng → sh ēng → shēng
shéng → sh éng → shéng
shěng → sh ěng → shěng
shèng → sh èng → shèng

二、听录音并熟读下面的句子。

Listen to the recording and read the following sentences till you learn them by heart.

1. Nǐ hǎo ma?
你 好 吗?

2. Wǒ hěn hǎo.
我 很 好。

3. Shēntǐ hǎo ma?
身体 好 吗?

4. Wǒ xià gè xīngqī qù zhōngguó.
我 下 个 星期 去 中国。

5. Tài hǎole!
太 好 了!

6. Hǎo jiǔ bú jiàn, nǐ máng ba?
好 久 不 见, 你 忙 吧?

7. Shēgyì zěnmeyàng?
生意 怎么样?

8. Mǎmǎhūhū.
马马虎虎。

三、跟读并辨别下面音节。

Read the following syllables and try to tell one from the other.

shēngyì—shēngyīn
shēntǐ—shēngqǐ
xīngqī—xīngqǐ
hǎojiǔ—hǎoqiú

四、请让我们一起再学习几个常用的词语，然后做练习。

Learn more useful words before you do the exercises.

补充词语 Supplementary Words

最近	zuìjìn	（名）	recent	(n.)
工作	gōngzuò	（名、动）	to work, job	(v.)(n.)
天气	tiānqì	（名）	weather	(n.)

选择填空 Fill in the Blanks with Appropriate Words

máng(忙)　hǎo(好)　hěn hǎo(很好)　zěnmeyàng(怎么样)

1. A：Nǐ zuìjìng gōngzuò máng ma?
   A：你 最近 工作 忙 吗?
   B：hěn
   B：很 ____________!

2. A：Zuìjìn shēntǐ ma?
   A：最近 身体 ____________ 吗?
   B：Hěn hǎo，xièxie!
   B：很 好，谢谢!

3. A：Zuìjìn nǐmen de shēngyì
   A：最近 你们 的 生意 ________?
   B：Hěn hǎo.
   B：很 好。

4. A：Zuìjìn de tiānqì zěnmeyàng?
   A：最近 的 天气 怎么样?
   B：____________。

五、请试着正确读出下面句子里“啊”的读音。

Read the following sentences with “a”, paying attention to the sound change of the particle.

1. Jīntiān zhēn máng a!
   今天 真 忙 啊!
   What a busy day today!

2. Zhè shì tā de jiā a!
这 是 他 的 家啊!
This is his home!

3. Diànnǎo duō hǎo a!
电脑 多 好 啊!
What a good computer this is!

4. Tā shì gōngsī de zhùlǐ a!
他 是 公司 的 助理 啊!
He is the assistant of the company.

六. 请试着给下面的词语加上拼音，并在右边的英文中找出相对应的解释。

Transliterate the following characters into *pinyin* and connect them with their corresponding English definition.

A. 马马虎虎　　1. week

B. 生意　　2. how

C. 怎么样　　3. China

D. 身体　　4. just so so

E. 星期　　5. business

F. 中国　　6. health

七、下面的情景用汉语你知道该怎么说吗？请试一试。

Try to express yourself in the following situations.

1. 你好久没有见到你的朋友了，刚见面时说什么？
How would you greet a friend you haven't seen for a long time?

2. 你的同事刚从外地回来，你用汉语向他表示问候。
How would you extend your greetings in Chinese to a colleague who has been away for some time?

3.你家里人从你们国家打来电话，你怎么用汉语先向他问候？

How would you start a telephone conversation with Chinese greetings when your family calls you from your home country?

八、汉字点击。

Open the CD to view the characters.

请通过光盘点击认读、书写下面的汉字。请注意汉字书写时的笔顺。

Open the CD, click the buttons, read and write the following characters, paying attention to their stroke-order.

啊 忙 身 体 星 期 中 国 怎 久 生 意 虎

自我评估 Self-assessment

1.你可以用汉语问候你的朋友了吧？

Can you exchange greetings with your friends in Chinese?

2.你还会用什么问候语？

Have you learned any other Chinese expressions for greeting apart from those provided in the text?

3.你认为汉语中的问候语是不是很简单？

Do you think Chinese expressions of amenity are easy to learn?

文化点击 Cultural Points

隐私 Privacy

如果你跟中国朋友聊天，你就会发现他们谈话的内容很随便，什么都可以说，什么都可以问，包括你的年龄、收入、婚姻状况等，都可能会问到。请你不要感到尴尬，因为他们并不是要了解你的隐私，而只是随便找一个话题，同时也表示他们对你的关心。有时见面他们还会问你“吃饭了吗？”“你去哪儿？”这都是打招呼，并不需要认真回答。

Among close Chinese friends the topic of conversation may be unlimited, varying from one’s age, income, marriage etc.. Don’t be embarrassed, as a matter of fact, they are not so interested in your personal secrets. Instead, they just want to show you their care by widening the topic. You don’t have to respond precisely when asked questions such as “chī fàn le ma” or “nǐ qù nǎr”.

Dì-shíbā kè　Bié zháojí
第 18 课　别 着急
Lesson 18　Don't Worry

导学 Guiding Remarks

当你要劝说别人不要做某件事情时，表达方式有很多。通过本课的学习，你将掌握几种常用的形式。

There are various Chinese expressions for giving advice. We will learn a few useful ones in this lesson.

A

Wang Guang goes on chatting with his customer.

Wáng Guāng：Nǐmen de xiàoyì zěnmeyàng?
王 光：你们 的 效益 怎么样?
Wang Guang：How is your business benefit?

Kèhù：Bù hǎo.
客户：不 好。
Customer：Very bad.

Wáng Guāng：Bié qiānxū le. Nǐmen de shēngyì yìzhí bú cuò.
王 光：别 谦虚了。你们 的 生意 一直 不 错。
Wang Guang：You are being too modest. I understand you've been doing well.

Kèhù：Zuìjìn bú tài hǎo. Wǒ zhèng zháojí ne.
客户：最近 不 太 好。我 正 着急 呢。
Customer：Below par these days. I am worried about it.

Wáng Guāng：Bié zháojí, huì hǎo de.
王 光：别 着急，会 好 的。
Wang Guang：Don't worry about it. You'll get it over soon.

B

Wang Guang comes into Li Lin's office with a camera in hand. He wants to take a picture of her.

Lǐ Lín：Bié pāi, bié pāi.
李 琳：别 拍，别 拍。
Li Lin：Stop! I don't want to have a picture taken.

With a click Xiao Wang captures her image. Looking at her affected posture on the screen of the digital camera they cannot but laugh.

Wáng Guāng: Bié máng le, xià bān le.
王 光：别 忙 了，下 班 了。
Wang Guang: Stop your work. It's time to knock off.

Li Lin looks up at the clock that says half past six.

Lǐ Lín: Ō. Xiè xie! Zhàopiàn shénme shíhou gěi wǒ?
李 琳：噢。谢谢！照片 什么 时候 给 我？
Li Lin: Thank you, but when can I get the picture?

Wáng Guāng: Bié zháojí, míngtiān jiù kě yǐ.
王 光：别 着急，明天 就 可以。
Wang Guang: Don't worry. It'll be ready tomorrow.

Lǐ Lín: Nǐ kě bié wàng le.
李 琳：你 可 别 忘 了。
Li Lin: Mind you don't forget it.

Wáng Guāng: Fàng xīn ba, bú huì wàng de.
王 光：放 心 吧，不 会 忘 的。
Wang Guang: No, I promise.

词 语 Word List

1.着急	zháojí	（动）	to worry about	*(v.)*
2.效益	xiàoyì	（名）	benefit	*(n.)*
3.谦虚	qiānxū	（形）	modest	*(adj.)*
4.一直	yì zhí	（副）	continuously	*(adv.)*
5.正	zhèng	（副）	in process of	*(adv.)*
6.拍	pāi	（动）	to take (a photo)	*(v.)*
7.班	bān	（名）	shift；class	*(n.)*
8.照片	zhàopiàn	（名）	photo	*(n.)*
9.时候	shíhou	（名）	time	*(n.)*
10.明天	míngtiān	（名）	tomorrow	*(n.)*
11.可	kě	（副）	be sure	*(adv.)*
12.忘	wàng	（动）	to forget	*(v.)*
13.放心	fàng xīn	（动）	to rest assured	*(v.)*

语言点链接 Language Points

1.“正……呢” The usage of “zhèng...ne”

“正……呢”表示正在进行的动作或状态。常和“现在”、“最近”等一起用。例如：“我现在正忙呢。”“他最近正在做这件事呢。”

“zhèng...ne” can be used together with “xiànzài” or “zuìjìn”, indicating an act in progress or a state. E.g. “wǒ xiànzài zhèng máng ne”, “tā zuìjìn zhèngzài zuò zhè jiàn shì ne”.

2.“不”和“别”的区别： The difference between “bù” and “bié”

汉语中“不”和“别”都表示否定，它们都可以放在动词的前面，在大多数情况下，“不”表示判断或拒绝，“别”表示劝阻和制止。当“别”表示劝阻时，用“别……了”的格式，当“别”单独用时表示制止。例如：

他不来了。	（判断）
我不去。	（拒绝）
他不是小王。	（判断）

你别走了。 (劝阻)

你们别去了。 (劝阻)

别喝那么多咖啡了。 (劝阻)

别，你先来吧。 (制止)

Both "bù" and "bié" are Chinese negatives, and are always followed by a verb. In most cases "bù" indicates one's judgement or refusal, while "bié" carries the sense of "advise someone not to do something" as in "bié... le". When used before a verb "bié" indicates the determent. E.g..

Tā bù lái le. (判断)
He is not coming. (judgement)

Wǒ bú qù. (拒绝)
I don't want to go. (refusal)

Tā bú shì xiǎo wáng. (判断)
He's not Xiao Wang. (judgement)

Nǐ bié zǒu le. (劝阻)
You are not supposed to leave. (dissuasion)

Nǐmen bié qù le. (劝阻)
You are not supposed to go. (dissuasion)

Bié hē nàme duō kāfēi le. (劝阻)
Don't drink so much coffee. (dissuasion)

Bié, Nǐ xiān lái ba. (制止)
No, after you. (determent)

"不要"也表示劝阻。例如：

你不要喝那么多咖啡了。 (劝阻)

"bú yào" also expresses one's dissuasion. E.g.

Nǐ bú yào hē nàme duō kāfēi le. (劝阻)
Don't drink that much coffee! (dissuasion)

练　习　Exercises

一、请听录音或跟着老师读。

Listen to the recording or read after the teacher.

qiān → q iān → qiān
qián → q ián → qián
qiǎn → q iǎn → qiǎn
qiàn → q iàn → qiàn

xū → x ū → xū
xú → x ú → xú
xǔ → x ǔ → xǔ
xù → x ù → xù

zuī → z uī → zuī
zuǐ → z uǐ → zuǐ
zuì → z uì → zuì

zhāo → zh āo → zhāo
zháo → zh áo → zháo
zhǎo → zh ǎo → zhǎo
zhào → zh ào → zhào

piān → p iān → piān
pián → p ián → pián
piǎn → p iǎn → piǎn
piàn → p iàn → piàn

pāi → p āi → pāi
pái → p ái → pái
pǎi → p ǎi → pǎi
pài → p ài → pài

hōu → h ōu → hōu
hóu → h óu → hóu
hǒu → h ǒu → hǒu
hòu → h òu → hòu

míng → m íng → míng
mǐng → m ǐng → mǐng
mìng → m ìng → mìng

fāng → f āng → fāng
fáng → f áng → fáng
fǎng → f ǎng → fǎng
fàng → f àng → fàng

xīn → x īn → xīn
xín → x ín → xín
xìn → x ìn → xìn

二、听录音并熟读下面的句子。

Listen to the recording and read the following sentences till you learn them by heart.

1. Nǐmen de xiàoyì zěnmeyàng?
   你们 的 效益 怎么样？

2. Bié qiānxū le. Nǐmen de shēngyì yìzhí bú cuò.
   别 谦虚 了。 你们 的 生意 一直 不 错。

3. Bié zháojí huì hǎo de.
   别 着急， 会 好 的。

4. Bié máng le, xià bān le.
   别 忙 了，下 班 了。

5. Bié zháojí, míngtiān jiù kěyǐ.
   别 着急， 明天 就 可以。

6. Nǐ kě bié wàng le.
   你 可 别 忘 了。

三、跟读并辨别下面音节。

Read the following syllables and try to tell one from the other.

zháojí—zǎoqǐ
míngtiān—níngyuàn
qiānxū—biānqū
xiàoyì—qiàopí

四、请让我们一起再学习几个常用的词语，然后做练习。

Learn more useful words before you do the exercises.

补充词语 Supplementary Words

担心	dānxīn	（动）	to worry	*(v.)*
生气	shēng qì		to get angry	

选择填空 Fill in the Blanks with Appropriate Words

hǎo(好)　　bù(不)　　zháojí(着急)

1. A：Nǐ zuìjìn de shēntǐ zěnmeyàng?
   A：你 最近 的 身体 怎么样？
   B：Bù
   B：不 __________！
   A：Bié dānxīn, huì hǎo de.
   A：别 担心，会 好 的。

2. A：Zuìjìn de shēngyì zěnmeyàng?
   A：最近 的 生意 怎么样？
   B：Bú tài hǎo.
   B：不 太 好。
   A：Bié
   A：别 __________。

3. A：Nǐ de gōngzuò shùnlì ma?
   A：你 的 工作 顺利 吗？
   B：　　　　shùnlì.
   B：__________ 顺利。
   A：Bié zháojí, huì hǎo de.
   A：别 着急，会 好 的。

4. A：Nǐ zěnme　　　　gāoxìng?
   A：你 怎么 __________ 高兴？
   B：Lǎobǎn pīpíng　　le wǒ.
   B：老板　批评(criticise)了 我。
   A：Bié shēng qì.
   A：别 生 气。

五、请试着在下面的句子里正确加上"别"和"不"。

Fill in the following blanks with an appropriate negative from 别 and 不.

1. 　　yòng le, wǒ zìjǐ lái.
   (　　) 用 了，我 自己 来。

2. Nǐ　　　zǒu.
你（　　）走。

3. 　　yòng kèqi.
（　　）用　客气。

4. Wǒ　　　hē kāfēi.
我（　　）喝 咖啡。

5. Nǐmen　　zuò.
你们（　　）坐。

6. Nǐmen　　lái le.
你们（　　）来了。

六、请试着给下面的词语加上拼音，并在右边的英文中找出相对应的解释。

Transliterate the following characters into *pinyin* and connect them with their corresponding English definition.

A. 老板　　　　(1) recently

B. 高兴　　　　(2) to take care of

C. 最近　　　　(3) benefit

D. 照顾　　　　(4) boss

E. 效益　　　　(5) glad

七、下面的情景用汉语你知道该怎么说吗？请试一试。

Try to express yourself in the following situations.

1. 你的朋友正在做一件很危险的事，你赶快阻止他。
Try to stop your friend from doing something dangerous.

2. 你的朋友不打算继续学习汉语了，你想办法劝他学下去。
Try to advise your friend not to give up his Chinese study.

3.你的朋友正为公司的效益不好而苦恼，你用汉语劝劝他。

Advise your friend not to worry about the low benefit of the company.

八、汉字点击。

Open the CD to view the characters.

请通过光盘点击认读、书写下面的汉字。请注意汉字书写时的笔顺。

Open the CD, click the buttons, read and write the following characters, paying attention to their stroke-order.

效　益　谦　虚　直　最　近　正　着　急

拍　照　班　时　候　明　忘　放　心

自我评估 Self-assessment

1.现在你学会劝解别人了吧?

What are the Chinese expressions you have learned for giving advice?

2.你可以和客户用汉语交谈吗?

How well can you talk with your customer in Chinese?

3.你估计中国人会给你的发音打多少分?

What marks will your Chinese colleagues give you for your Chinese pronunciation?

文化点击 Cultural Points

中国人送礼的习惯　Gift Exchange among the Chinese People

无论是私人交往还是商业活动，都免不了礼尚往来。中国人一般会送一些纪念品，以表达友好的感情。中国人所送的礼品比较重视实用性，可能都是你的生活中可以用到的。如果是朋友之间赠送礼品，一般不送梨、伞等，对老年人，特别是祝寿时，是万万不可送钟的。

Gift exchange is common in personal or business communication. Chinese people often present souvenirs to one another as a reminder of their friendship. Generally they are concerned about the usefulness of the gifts, ranging from daily necessities to other small items. Pears and umbrellas are taboo as gifts to friends. Customarily clocks may, if sent as a birthday gift to aged people, elicit ill feelings.

Dì-shíjiǔ kè Wèi yǒuyì gān bēi
第 19 课 为友谊干杯
Lesson 19 To Our Friendship

导学 Guiding Remarks

在商务活动中，你一定会参加各种形式的酒会，在酒会上，热情好客的中国人会说什么呢？请通过下面的场景来了解一下，记住几句常用的句子，会使你在这种活动中应对自如。

Feasts and cocktail parties are social occasions for business men to socialize and befriend others. What would the hospitable Chinese say to one another at such gatherings? In the following situational dialogues you are going to learn some useful sentences that will help you to fit in and respond appropriately.

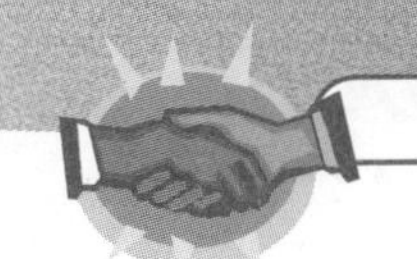

A

A Pre-New-Year gathering is arranged for old and new customers. On behalf of the company Mike proposes a toast to each guest.

Màikè：Wǒ tí yì, wèi wǒmen de yǒuyì gān bēi!
麦克：我 提 议，为 我们 的 友谊 干 杯！
Mike：Allow me to propose a toast for our friendship!

Dàjiā：Gān bēi!
大家：干 杯！
Everybody：Cheers!

Màikè：Wèi wǒmen hézuò yúkuài gān bēi!
麦克：为 我们 合作 愉快 干 杯！
Mike：Here's to our happy cooperation!

Dàijiā：Gān bēi!
大家：干 杯！
Everybody：Cheers!

Mike comes to a senior customer.

Màikè：Wǒ jìng nín yì bēi，zhù nín shēntǐ jiànkāng!
麦克：我 敬 您 一 杯，祝 您 身体 健康!
Mike：Here's to your health!

Kèhù：Xièxie! Wǒ yě jìng nǐ yì bēi，zhù nǐ fā cái!
客户：谢谢! 我 也 敬 你 一 杯，祝 你 发 财!
Customer：Thank you! And to your health. Wish you prosperity!

Màikè：Zhù nín fā cái!
麦克：祝 您 发 财!
Mike：A prosperous business to you!

Kèhù：Yìqǐ fā cái!
客户：一起 发 财!
Customer：Let's make a pile!

Màikè：Yìqǐ fā cái! Gān bēi!
麦克：(smiling)一起 发 财! 干 杯!
Mike：Everybody gets rich! Cheers!

Kèhù：Gān bēi!
客户：干 杯!
Customer：Cheers!

B

John returns to Beijing. Mike and Li Lin hold a party in his honour.

Màikè：Jīn wǎn wǒmen wèi nǐ jiēfēng，huānyíng nǐ.
麦克：今 晚 我们 为 你 接风， 欢迎 你。(Raising his glass.)
Mike：Tonight's dinner of welcome is given in your honour. Welcome!

John：Xièxie! Nǐ tài kèqi le.
John：谢谢! 你 太 客气 了。(Raising his glass.)
John：Thank you! How nice of you.

They join one another in raising their glasses.

Lǐ Lín：Huānyíng nǐ zài cì guānglín.
李 琳：欢迎 你 再 次 光临。
Li Lin：Welcome back！ It's our honour to have your renewed participation.

John：Xièxie！
John：谢谢！（They raise their glasses.）
John：Thank you！

Màikè：Lái，gān yì bēi！
麦克：来，干 一 杯！
Mike：John，Cheers！

John：Hǎo，gān bēi！
John：好，干 杯！
John：Mike，cheers！

Màikè：Gān bēi！
麦克：干 杯！
Mike：To all！

Lǐ Lín：Gān bēi！
李 琳：干 杯！
Li Lin：To everyone！

词 语 Word List

1.为	wèi	（介）	for	*(prep.)*
2.友谊	yǒuyì	（名）	friendship	*(n.)*
3.干杯	gān bēi		to drink a toast	
4.提议	tí yì	（动）	to propose	*(v.)*
5.合作	hézuò	（动）	to cooperate	*(v.)*
6.敬	jìng	（动）	to drink to (your health)	*(v.)*
7.健康	jiànkāng	（名、形）	health；healthy	*(n.,adv.)*
8.发财	fā cái	（动）	to get rich	*(v.)*
9.一起	yìqǐ	（副）	together	*(adv.)*
10.今晚	jīn wǎn		tonight	
11.接风	jiēfēng	（动）	to give a dinner of welcome	*(v.)*
12.次	cì	（量）	(a measure word)	*(mw.)*
13.光临	guānglín	（动）	to visit (of a guest)	*(v.)*

语言点链接 Language Points

时间名词（1） Nominal Time Words

汉语中常用的时间名词有很多，下面介绍一些常用的。

There are a great number of nouns in Chinese. The following are commonly used nominal time words.

汉 语	拼 音	英 译
今天	jīntiān	today
明天	míngtiān	tomorrow
后天	hòutiān	the day after tomorrow
大后天	dà hòutiān	three days from today
昨天	zuótiān	yesterday
前天	qiántiān	the day before yesterday
大前天	dà qiántiān	two days before yesterday
上星期	shàng xīngqī	Last week
下星期	xià xīngqī	next week
今年	jīnnián	this week

去年	qùnián	last year
明年	míngnián	next year
前年	qiánnián	the year before last

练　习　Exercises

一、请听录音或跟着老师读。

Listen to the recording or read after the teacher.

gān → g　ān → gān
gǎn → g　ǎn → gǎn
gàn → g　àn → gàn

bēi → b　ēi → bēi
běi → b　ěi → běi
bèi → b　èi → bèi

yōu → y　ōu → yōu
yóu → y　óu → yóu
yǒu → y　ǒu → yǒu
yòu → y　òu → yòu

zuō → z　uō → zuō
zuó → z　uó → zuó
zuǒ → z　uǒ → zuǒ
zuò → z　uò → zuò

kāng → k　āng → kāng
káng → k　áng → káng
kàng → k　àng → kàng

fā → f　ā → fā
fá → f　á → fá
fǎ → f　ǎ → fǎ
fà → f　à → fà

cāi → c　āi → cāi
cái → c　ái → cái
cǎi → c　ǎi → cǎi
cài → c　ài → cài

wān → w　ān → wān
wán → w　án → wán
wǎn → w　ǎn → wǎn
wàn → w　àn → wàn

cī → c　ī → cī
cí → c　í → cí
cǐ → c　ǐ → cǐ
cì → c　ì → cì

二、听录音并熟读下面的句子。

Listen to the recording, read the following sentences till you learn them by heart.

1. Wǒ tí yì, wèi wǒmen de yǒuyì gān bēi!
我 提 议，为 我们 的 友谊 干 杯！

2. Wèi wǒmen hézuò yúkuài gān bēi!
为 我们 合作 愉快 干 杯！

3. Wǒ jìng nín yì bēi, zhù nín shēntǐ jiànkāng!
我 敬 您 一 杯，祝 您 身体 健康！

4. Wǒ yě jìng nǐ yì bēi, zhù nǐ fā cái!
我 也 敬 你 一 杯，祝 你 发 财！

5. Jīn wǎn wǒmen wèi nǐ jiēfēng.
今 晚 我们 为 你 接风。

6. Huānyíng nǐ zài cì guānglín.
欢迎 你 再 次 光临。

7. Gān bēi!
干 杯！

三、跟读并辨别下面音节。

Read the following syllables and try to tell one from the other.

gānbēi–gāngbēi
guānglín–guānlǐ
jiànkāng–jiànggāng
jiēfēng–qiēfēn

四、请让我们一起再学习几个常用的词语，然后做练习。

Learn more useful words before you do the exercises.

补充词语 Supplementary Words

美好	měihǎo	（形）	bright	*(adj.)*
未来	wèilái	（名）	future	*(n.)*
洗尘	xǐchén	（动）	to give a dinner of welcome to a visitor from afar	*(v.)*

选择填空 Fill in the Blanks with Appropriate Words

gān bēi(干杯)　　xièxie(谢谢)　　yǒuyì(友谊)

1. A：Wǒ tí yì, wèi wǒmen de měihǎo wèilái gān bēi!
   A：我 提 议，为 我们 的 美好 未来 干 杯！
   B：________________！

2. A：Jīntiān wǒmen wèi nǐ jiēfēng xǐchén.
   A：今天 我们 为 你 接风 洗尘。
   B：________________。

3. A：Wèi　　　　　　　gān bēi!
   A：为________________干 杯！
   B：Gān bēi!
   B：干 杯！

4. A：Wèi nǐ de guānglín gān bēi!
   A：为 你 的 光临 干 杯！
   B：________________！

五、请根据已知条件填表格。

Fill in the the following blanks based on the information given.

今天 jīntiān	5月(yuè)3日(rì)	去年 qùnián		星期一 xīngqīyī	
昨天 zuótiān		今年 jīnnián	2005年(nián)	星期六 xīngqīliù	
明天 míngtiān		明年 míngnián		上星期日 shàng xīngqīrì	
前天 qiántiān		前年 qiánnián		星期二 xīngqīèr	6月(yuè) 21日(rì)

六、请试着给下面的词语加上拼音，并在右边的英文中找出相对应的解释。

Transliterate the following sentences into *pinyin* and connect them with the corresponding English definition.

A.欢迎光临! (1) To our friendship!

B.为友谊干杯! (2) Wish you prosperity!

C.祝你发财! (3) How kind you are!

D.你太客气了。 (4) Welcome!

七、下面的情景用汉语你知道该怎么说吗？请试一试。

Try to express yourself in the following situations.

1.在新年联欢会上，你用汉语为大家祝酒。
Drink a toast in Chinese at a New Year party.

2.在朋友的生日宴会上，请用汉语对他说祝福的话。
Wish your friend a happy birthday in Chinese at his birthday party.

3.老朋友聚会，你用汉语为大家祝酒。
Propose a toast in Chinese at a reunion party of old friends.

八、汉字点击。

Open the CD to view the characters.

请通过光盘点击认读、书写下面的汉字。请注意汉字书写时的笔顺。

Open the CD, click the buttons, read and write the following Chinese characters, focusing your attention on their stroke-order.

提 议 干 杯 友 谊 合 敬 健
康 发 财 起 晚 接 风 次 临

自我评估 Self-assessment

1. 你对在大庭广众下说汉语有自信吗?
Are you a confident speaker of Chinese on a public occasion?

2. 你已经会用汉语说祝酒辞了吗?
Are you able to propose a toast in Chinese?

3. 你已经学会了多少汉字。
How many Chinese characters have you learned?

文化点击 Cultural Points

关于干杯 What is meant by "cheers" in Chinese

干杯的本意是把杯中的酒喝干，但在比较正式的场合，一般情况下，并不是一定要喝干杯中的酒，只要举起杯子喝一口就可以了，其实这只是一种形式。在一些比较熟悉的人聚餐的场合，中国人为了表示热情和友好，会要求你喝光杯里的酒，这时候会说："干了！"你自己要根据情况决定是否喝光，如果你喝干了一杯，随后中国人会要求你再干一杯，这样的情况可能会重复下去。所以，你如果不能喝很多酒，或者不想喝，你要表示自己的酒量不行，不能喝很多，可以要求少喝一点，比如喝一半、一点，并表示抱歉。

The Chinese equivalent to "cheers"(gān bēi) is "drink up every drop given" or "empty one's glass". However on formal occasions one may propose a toast by drinking spirits in sips, rather than gulps if one is not a heavy drinker. At an informal party acquaintances often encourage one another to drink their fill by saying "gān le" (let's drink it up). This is generally understood as an expression of friendship and hospitality. One may drink it up if one has a good capacity for liquor. Thus the drinking may go on round by round. If one is a light drinker or doesn't want to drink any more, one may take a small sip, drink half of it, or quit with an apology.

Dì-èrshí kè Jiérì kuàilè
第 20 课 节日快乐
Lesson 20 A Happy Festival to You

导学 Guiding Remarks

在节日里或朋友有喜庆的事情时，我们习惯表示一下祝贺和祝愿。如果你能用汉语对你的中国朋友表示一下你的祝福，他会非常高兴的，并且还会增进你们之间的友谊。

We offer a friend our congratulations upon his success or extend our good wishes to him during a particular festival. If you are able to send your Chinese friend a festive message in Chinese, he would be very happy to receive it, and your friendship would be redoubled.

课文 Text

A

Wang Guang comes to the company in excitement.

Wáng Guāng：Dàjiā hǎo!
王　光：大家 好!
Wang Guang：Hello，everybody!

Lǐ Lín：Zěnme zhème gāoxìng?
李　琳：怎么　这么　高兴?
Li Lin：What's all this excitement about?

Wáng Guāng：
王　光：(With a mysterious and complacent smile he pats his folder)
Shēngyì tánchéng le!
生意　谈成　了!
Wang Guang：I've got a deal!

Lǐ Lín：Shìma? Gōngxǐ! Gōngxǐ!
李　琳：是吗?　恭喜!　恭喜!
Li Lin：Have you? Congratulations!

Hearing the news A and B come over to join them.

Tóngshì: Xiǎo Wáng, gōngxǐ nǐ! Zhùhè nǐ!
同事A、B:(Patting him on the back)小王,恭喜你!祝贺你!
A and B: Xiao Wang, congratulations! That's great!

Wáng Guāng: Màizǒng zài ma?
王光:(To Li)麦总在吗?
Wang Guang: Is Maizong in?

Lǐ Lín: Zài.
李琳:在。
Li Lin: Yes, he is.

Wáng Guāng: Màizǒng, Shànghǎi de nà bǐ shēngyì tánchéng le.
王光:(Entering Maizong's office)麦总,上海的那笔生意谈成了。
Wang Guang: Maizong, I've got the deal from Shanghai.

Màikè: Shì ma? Tài hǎo le! Hétong qiān le ma?
麦克:是吗?太好了!合同签了吗?
Mike: Have you? Great! Have you signed the contract?

Wáng Guāng: Qiān le. Gěi, nǐ kàn.
王光:签了。(Taking out the document from his folder)给,你看。
Wang Guang: Yes, we have. Here you are.

Màikè: A, tài hǎo le! Xiǎo Wáng. Zhùhè nǐ!
麦克:(Glancing over the contract)啊,太好了!小王。(Shaking hands with him)祝贺你。
Mike: Ah, well done, Xiao Wang. Congratulations!

B

Mike is making an announcement to the employees in the hall.

Màikè：Gè wèi, míngtiān shì Shèngdàn Jié, gōngsī fàng jià
麦克：各 位，明天 是 圣诞 节，公司 放 假
sān tiān, bù, sān tiān bàn! Jīntiān xiàwǔ kāishǐ.
三 天，不，三 天 半！ 今天 下午 开始。
Mike：May I have your attention please, everybody! It will be Christmas Day tomorrow. We'll have three days off, oh, no, I meant to say we would have three and a half days off from this afternoon onwards.

Dàjiā：Ō——, hǎo, hǎo, tài hǎo le! Xièxie! Xièxie Màizǒng!
大家：(Clapping)噢——，好，好，太 好 了！谢谢！谢谢 麦总！
Everybody：Ah, that's great. Thank you, Maizong!

Wáng Guāng：Màizǒng, nín zài nǎr guò Shèngdàn Jié?
王 光：麦总， 您 在 哪儿 过 圣诞 节？
Wang Guang：Where will you have your Christmas, Maizong?

Màikè：Wǒ qù Xiānggǎng, jīntiān xiàwǔ zǒu.
麦克：我 去 香港， 今天 下午 走。
Mike：I'm going to Hong Kong. I'm leaving this afternoon.

Wáng Guāng：Nà zhù nín Shèngdàn kuàilè!
王　光：那祝您圣诞快乐！
Wang Guang：I wish you a merry Christmas!

Màikè：Xièxie! Shèngdàn kuàilè! Zhù dàjiā jiérì yúkuài!
麦克：谢谢。圣诞快乐！(To everybody)祝大家节日愉快！
Mike：Thank you. A merry Christmas to you all! Enjoy yourselves!

Dàjiā：Xièxie! Zhù Màizǒng Shèngdàn kuàilè!
大家：(One after another) 谢谢，祝麦总圣诞快乐！
Jiérì yúkuài!
节日愉快！
Everybody：Thank you, Maizong! Wish you a merry Christmas! Wishing you the season's best!

词　语　Word List

1.节日	jiérì	（名）	festival	*(n.)*
2.快乐	kuàilè	（形）	happy	*(adj.)*
3.这么	zhème	（副）	such, so	*(adv.)*
4.谈	tán	（动）	to chat, to talk	*(v.)*
5.成	chéng	（动）	to succeed	*(v.)*
6.恭喜	gōngxǐ	（动）	to congratulate	*(v.)*
7.祝贺	zhùhè	（动）	to congratulate	*(v.)*
8.笔	bǐ	（量）	(a measure word)	*(mw.)*
9.合同	hétong	（名）	contract	*(n.)*
10.各位	gè wèi	（代）	everybody	*(pron.)*
11.放假	fàng jià		to have a holiday	
12.半	bàn	（数）	half	*(num.)*
13.下午	xiàwǔ	（名）	afternoon	
14.过	guò	（动）	to keep	*(v.)*
15.圣诞节	Shèngdàn Jié	（专名）	Christmas	*(pn.)*
16.上海	Shànghǎi	（专名）	Shanghai	*(pn.)*
17.香港	Xiānggǎng	（专名）	Hongkong	*(pn.)*

语言点链接　Language Points

1.时间名词（2） Time Words

汉语里表示一天中时间的词语也有很多，下面介绍几个：

There are time words for different parts of the day in Chinese. They are：

汉　语	拼　音	英　译
上午	shàngwǔ	Morning（8–12 am）
早上	zǎoshang	early morning
早晨	zǎochén	early morning
下午	xiàwǔ	afternoon
晚上	wǎnshang	Evening
夜晚	yèwǎn	Night

2.“各位”和“大家” “gè wèi” and “dàjiā”

“各位”和“大家”都是代词，但“各位”可以用做称谓，“大家”不能用做称谓。

Both “gè wèi” and “dàjiā” are pronouns, but the former may serve as an appellation, and the latter can not.

3.时量词 Time Measure Words

表示时间经历的长短的量词叫时量词。时量词和动量词一样，放在动词的后面表示动作所经历的时间。例如：“放假三天”。补充说明“放”的动作经历三天。也可以把动词后面的名词放在时间词的后面，即：“放三天假”。

Time words that can be used to indicate the length of time are known as time measure words. Just like verbal measure words, they are often placed after verbs to show the length of time. E.g. In“fàng jià sān tiān”,“sān tiān” functioning as a complement indicates the length of time. Grammatically the noun after the verb “fàng” may be put at the end of the phrase, namely “fàng sān tiān jià”.

4.“是吗？” The Usage of “shì ma”

“是吗？”并不表示疑问，而是表示惊喜，有时表示一种应付。

“shì ma” is not a question. Instead it carries a sense of surprise, or can be used as an echo in a dialogue between two people.

练　习　Exercises

一、请听录音或跟着老师读。

Listen to the recording or read after the teacher.

tān → t ān → tān　　chēng → ch ēng → chēng
tán → t án → tán　　chéng → ch éng → chéng
tǎn → t ǎn → tǎn　　chěng → ch ěng → chěng
tàn → t àn → tàn　　chèng → ch èng → chèng

xī → x ī → xī　　bī → b ī → bī
xí → x í → xí　　bí → b í → bí
xǐ → x ǐ → xǐ　　bǐ → b ǐ → bǐ
xì → x ì → xì　　bì → b ì → bì

dān → d ān → dān　　gāng → g āng → gāng
dǎn → d ǎn → dǎn　　gǎng → g ǎng → gǎng
dàn → d àn → dàn　　gàng → g àng → gàng

二、听录音并熟读下面的句子。

Listen to the recording and read the following sentences till you learn them by heart.

1. Zěnme zhème gāoxìng?
怎么　这么　高兴?

2. Gōngxǐ nǐ! Zhùhè nǐ!
恭喜　你!　祝贺　你!

3. Shànghǎi de nà bǐ shēngyì tánchéng le.
上海　的 那 笔　生意　谈成　了。

4. Hétong qiān le ma?
合同　签 了 吗?

5. Gè wèi, míngtiān shì Shèngdàn Jié, gōngsī fàng jià sān tiān.
各 位,　明天　是　圣诞　节,　公 司 放 假 三 天。

6. Nín zài nǎr guò Shèngdàn Jié?
 您 在 哪儿 过 圣诞 节?

7. Zhù nín Shèngdàn kuàilè!
 祝 您 圣诞 快乐!

8. Zhù dàjiā jiérì yúkuài!
 祝 大家 节日 愉快!

三、跟读并辨别下面音节。

Read the following syllables and try to tell one from the other.

hétong—wūtóng
jiàrì—jiérì
fàngjià—fàngxià
gōngxǐ—gōngjǐ

四、请让我们一起再学习几个常用的词语，然后做练习。

Learn more useful words before you do the exercises.

补充词语 Supplementary Words

生日	shēngrì	(名)	birthday	*(n.)*
新年	xīnnián	(名)	New Year	*(n.)*

选择填空 Fill in the Blanks with Appropriate Words

Xièxie(谢谢) yě(也) kuàilè(快乐)

1. A：Zhù nín shēngrì kuàilè!
 A：祝 您 生日 快乐!
 B：________________!

2. A：Zhù nǐ xīnnián yúkuài!
 A：祝 你 新年 愉快!
 B：   zhù nǐ xīnnián yúkuài!
 B：________________祝 你 新年 愉快!

3. A：Jiérì
A：节日 ________________！
B：Jiérì kuàilè!
B：节日 快 乐！

4. A：Gōngxǐ fā cái!
A：恭喜 发 财！
B：____________________！

五、在下面句子的________里添上“各位”或“大家”（可以选两个）。

Fill in the following blanks with “gè wèi” or “dàjiā” (or both if appropriate).

(1) qǐng zuò hǎo.
________，请 坐 好。

(2) Qǐng zuò hǎo.
请________坐 好。

(3) nǐmen zài nǎr guò Shèngdàn Jié?
________，你们 在 哪儿 过 圣诞 节？

(4) zài nǎr guò Shèngdàn Jié?
________在 哪儿 过 圣诞 节？

六、请试着给下面的词语加上拼音，并在右边的英文中找出相对应的解释。

Put the following sentences into Chinese pinyin and connect them with the equivalent English：

A. 圣诞快乐！	Hétong qiān le ma?	1. Have you signed your contract?
B. 合同签了吗？	Zěnme zhème gāoxìng?	2. Congratulations!
C. 怎么这么高兴？	Gōngxǐ nǐ!	3. Merry Christmas!
D. 恭喜你！	Shèngdàn kuàilè!	4. What's all this excitement about?

七、下面的情景用汉语你知道该怎么说吗？请试一试。

Try to express yourself in the following situations.

1.新年到了，请用汉语向你的朋友表示新年祝福。
Send New Year greetings in Chinese to your friends.

2.今天是你朋友的生日，请用汉语对他说祝福的话。
Say "Happy Birthday" in Chinese to your friend whose birthday is today.

3.圣诞节的早上，见到你的朋友后，用汉语对他表示祝贺。
Exchange festival greetings in Chinese with your friends on a Christmas morning.

八、汉字点击。

Open the CD to view the characters.

请通过光盘点击认读、书写下面的汉字。请注意汉字书写时的笔顺。

Open the CD, click the buttons, read and write the following Chinese characters, focusing your attention on their stroke-order.

谈　成　恭　喜　贺　海　笔　合　各　圣　诞
节　放　假　半　午　过　香　港　快　乐

自我评估 Self-assessment

1.学完全册书，你共用了多长时间？
How long did it take you to learn this textbook?

2.你认为本书中哪些内容对你最有用？
What do you think are the most useful parts of the book?

3.你是否愿意马上进入下一册的学习？
Are you going to study the follow-up textbook right now?

文化点击 Cultural Points

中国的节日　Chinese Festivals And Holidays

中国的节日有很多，传统节日中最重要的有春节（农历正月初一，公历大约在2月），此外，还有元宵节（农历正月十五，公历大约在2月中下旬到3月初之间）、清明节（公历大约4月3、4、5、6

日)、端午节（农历五月初五，公历大约6月)、中秋节（农历八月十五，公历大约9月中下旬到10月上旬之间)、重阳节（农历九月初九，公历大约10月下旬到11月上旬之间）等；纪念日有新年（公历1月1日)、妇女节（公历3月8日)、劳动节（公历5月1日)、儿童节（公历6月1日)、中国共产党诞生日（公历7月1日)、中国人民解放军建军纪念日（公历8月1日)、教师节（公历9月10日)、国庆节（公历10月1日）等等。

Of the traditional Chinese festivals the most important one is the Spring Festival (the 1st day of the 1st lunar month). In addition there are festivals such as the Lantern Festival (the 15th of the 1st lunar month), Tomb-sweeping Day (April 3,4,5,6, observed as a festival for worshiping at ancestral graves), the Dragon Boat Festival (the 5th day of the 5th lunar month), the Mid-autumn Festival (the 15th day of the 8th lunar month), the Double Ninth Festival (the 9th day of the 9th lunar month). The commemoration days are the New Year's Day (January 1), Women's Day (March 8), Labour Day (May 1), Children's Day (June 1), the Anniversary of the founding of the Communist Party of China (July 1), Army Day (August 1), Teachers' Day (September 10), and National Day (October 1).

词语索引

Vocabulary

啊	a	(叹)	ah	(*int.*)	(3)
哎	āi	(叹)	here	(*int.*)	(8)
爱人	àiren	(名)	wife or husband	(*n.*)	(7)
吧	ba	(语气)	(a modal particle)	(*mp.*)	(10)
班	bān	(名)	shift; class	(*n.*)	(18)
办公室	bàngōngshì	(名)	office	(*n.*)	(7)
半	bàn	(数)	half	(*num.*)	(20)
帮	bāng	(动)	to help	(*v.*)	(3)
帮忙	bāng máng		help		(11)
棒	bàng	(形)	good	(*adj.*)	(13)
保重	bǎozhòng	(形)	to take care	(*v.*)	(15)
报告	bàogào	(名)	report	(*n.*)	(16)
抱歉	bàoqiàn	(形)	sorry	(*adj.*)	(9)
北京	Běijīng	(专名)	Beijing	(*pn.*)	(5)
笔	bǐ	(量)	(a measure word)	(*mw.*)	(20)
别	bié	(副)	do not	(*adv.*)	(11)
不	bù	(副)	not	(*adv.*)	(3)
不错	bú cuò	(形)	not bad	(*adj.*)	(13)
不要紧	bú yàojǐn		It doesn't matter.		(9)
部	bù	(名)	section, department	(*n.*)	(7)
茶	chá	(名)	tea	(*n.*)	(6)
车	chē	(名)	car, bus	(*n.*)	(9)
成	chéng	(动)	to succeed	(*v.*)	(20)
吃	chī	(动)	to eat, to take	(*v.*)	(6)
抽烟	chōu yān		to smoke		(10)
传真	chuánzhēn	(名)	fax	(*n.*)	(8)
次	cì	(量)	(a measure word)	(*mw.*)	(19)
打扰	dǎrǎo	(动)	to disturb，to bother	(*v.*)	(16)
大家	dàjiā	(代)	everyone	(*pron.*)	(2)
担心	dānxīn	(动)	to worry	(*v.*)	(18)

到	dào	(动)	to arrive, also used as a complement	(*v.*)	(5)
的	de	(助)	of	(*aux.*)	(4)
等	děng	(动)	to wait	(*v.*)	(8)
递	dì	(动)	to pass on to	(*v.*)	(16)
电脑	diànnǎo	(名)	computer	(*n.*)	(8)
堵	dǔ	(动)	to jam, to be caught in a traffic jam	(*v.*)	(9)
对	duì	(形)	correct	(*adj.*)	(14)
对不起	duìbuqǐ		sorry		(9)
多	duō	(形)	many, more	(*adj.*)	(3)
发	fā	(动)	to send	(*v.*)	(8)
发财	fā cái		to get rich	(*v.*)	(19)
放假	fàng jià		to have a holiday		(20)
放心	fàng xīn	(动)	to rest assured	(*v.*)	(18)
非常	fēicháng	(副)	extremely	(*adv.*)	(3)
分别	fēnbié	(动)	to say good-bye, to separate	(*v.*)	(14)
服务员	fúwùyuán	(名)	waiter, person at sb's service	(*n.*)	(3)
干杯	gān bēi		to drink a toast		(19)
感谢	gǎnxiè	(动)	thank	(*v.*)	(3)
高兴	gāoxìng	(形)	glad	(*adj.*)	(5)
个	gè	(量)	(a measure word)	(*mw.*)	(3)
各位	gè wèi	(代)	everybody	(*pron.*)	(20)
给	gěi	(动)	to give, for, to	(*v.*)	(8)
工艺品	gōngyìpǐn	(名)	handicraft article	(*n.*)	(2)
工作	gōngzuò	(名、动)	to work, job	(*v.,n.*)	(17)
公司	gōngsī	(名)	company	(*n.*)	(4)
恭喜	gōngxǐ	(动)	to congratulate	(*v.*)	(20)
光临	guānglín	(动)	presence (of a guest, etc.)	(*v.*)	(5)
广东	Guǎngdōng	(专名)	name of a province	(*pn.*)	(4)
国	guó	(名)	country	(*n.*)	(14)
过	guò	(动)	to keep	(*v.*)	(20)

过	guò	（动）	to go through	(*v.*)	(16)
过奖	guòjiǎng	（动）	to overpraise	(*v.*)	(13)
过去	guòqu	（动）	to pass	(*v.*)	(16)
好	hǎo	（形）	good, nice	(*adj.*)	(2)
好久	hǎo jiǔ	（名）	long time	(*n.*)	(17)
喝	hē	（动）	to drink	(*v.*)	(6)
合同	hétong	（名）	contract	(*n.*)	(20)
合作	hézuò	（动）	to cooperate	(*v.*)	(19)
盒	hé	（量）	box	(*mw.*)	(8)
很	hěn	（副）	very	(*adv.*)	(5)
画面	huàmiàn	（名）	picture	(*n.*)	(13)
欢迎	huānyíng	（动）	to welcome	(*v.*)	(4)
还	hái	（副）	also	(*adv.*)	(17)
还是	háishì	（副）	had better, still	(*conj.*)	(12)
回	huí	（动）	to return	(*v.*)	(14)
会	huì	（动）	will	(*v.*)	(14)
惠顾	huìgù	（动）	patronize	(*v.*)	(5)
加	jiā	（动）	to add to	(*v.*)	(11)
见	jiàn	（动）	to see	(*v.*)	(5)
见面	jiàn miàn		to see, to meet		(14)
健康	jiànkāng	（名、形）	health; healthy	(*n.,adj.*)	(19)
交	jiāo	（动）	to hand, to submit	(*v.*)	(16)
接风	jiēfēng	（动）	to give a dinner of welcome	(*v.*)	(19)
节日	jiérì	（名）	festival		(20)
今天	jīntiān	（名）	today	(*n.*)	(16)
今晚	jīn wǎn		tonight		(19)
进	jìn	（动）	to come in	(*v.*)	(6)
进来	jìnlái	（动）	to come in	(*v.*)	(10)
经理	jīnglǐ	（名）	manager	(*n.*)	(4)
敬	jìng	（动）	to drink to (your health)	(*v.*)	(19)
就	jiù	（副）	right now	(*adv.*)	(14)
咖啡	kāfēi	（名）	coffee	(*n.*)	(11)
可	kě	（副）	be sure	(*adv.*)	(18)

可以	kěyǐ	(动)	can, able	(v.)	(8)
客户	kēhù	(名)	client, customer, user	(n.)	(5)
客气	kēqi	(形)	polite	(adj.)	(3)
快乐	kuàilē	(形)	happy	(adj.)	(20)
来	lái	(动)	to come	(v.)	(4)
来	lái	(动)	to let	(v.)	(12)
老板	lǎobǎn	(名)	boss, manager	(n.)	(7)
李琳	Lǐ Lín	(专名)	name of a person	(pn.)	(2)
里	lǐ	(名)	inside, in	(n.)	(9)
了	le	(助)	used after a verb or verbal phrase to indicate the co-mpletion of a real or exp-ected action or a change	(aux.)	(9)
刘力	Liú Lì	(专名)	name of a person	(pn.)	(4)
留步	liú bù	(动)	don't bother to come any further	(v.)	(15)
旅途	lǚtú	(名)	trip	(n.)	(15)
麻烦	máfan	(动)	to trouble	(v.)	(16)
马马虎虎	mǎmǎhūhū	(形)	just so so	(adj.)	(17)
吗	ma	(语气)	(a final interrogative particle)	(mp.)	(10)
买	mǎi	(动)	to buy	(v.)	(8)
麦克	Màikē	(专名)	Mike	(pn.)	(2)
忙	máng	(名)	help	(n.)	(3)
忙	máng	(形)	busy	(adj.)	(17)
没关系	méi guānxi		never mind		(9)
没事儿	méi shìr		not serious, never mind		(9)
美	měi	(形)	beautiful	(adj.)	(13)
美好	měihǎo	(形)	bright	(adj.)	(19)
们	men		(suffix for plurality)		(2)
秘书	mìshū	(名)	secretary	(n.)	(7)
名片	míngpiàn	(名)	visiting card	(n.)	(8)
明天	míngtiān	(名)	tomorrow	(n.)	(18)
拿	ná	(动)	to take	(v.)	(16)

哪里	nǎli	(代)	not at all, where	(*pron.*)	(15)
奶	nǎi	(名)	milk	(*n.*)	(11)
呢	ne	(语气)	(a final interrogative particle)	(*mp.*)	(9)
能	néng	(动)	can, to be able	(*v.*)	(10)
能干	nénggàn		capable	(*adj.*)	(13)
你	nǐ	(代)	you (singular)	(*pron.*)	(2)
您	nín	(代)	you (a polite form)	(*pron.*)	(2)
噢	ō	(叹)	oh	(*int.*)	(2)
拍	pāi	(动)	to take (a photo)	(*v.*)	(18)
朋友	péngyou	(名)	friend	(*n.*)	(7)
平安	píng'ān	(形)	safe	(*adj.*)	(15)
谦虚	qiānxū	(形)	modest	(*adj.*)	(18)
签字	qiān zì	(名)	signature	(*n.*)	(7)
请	qǐng	(动)	please, to invite, to ask	(*v.*)	(6)
请客	qǐng kè		to stand treat		(13)
去	qù	(动)	to go	(*v.*)	(17)
认识	rènshi	(动)	to know	(*v.*)	(7)
软盘	ruǎnpán	(名)	software	(*n.*)	(10)
上	shàng	(动)	to go up	(*v.*)	(12)
上海	Shànghǎi	(专名)	Shanghai	(*pn.*)	(20)
身体	shēntǐ	(名)	body	(*n.*)	(17)
生气	shēng qì		to get angry		(18)
生日	shēngrì	(名)	birthday	(*n.*)	(20)
生意	shēngyì	(名)	business	(*n.*)	(17)
声音	shēngyīn	(名)	sound	(*n.*)	(13)
圣诞节	Shèngdàn Jié	(专名)	Christmas	(*pn.*)	(20)
什么	shénme	(代)	what	(*pron.*)	(16)
时候	shíhou	(名)	time	(*n.*)	(18)
事	shì	(名)	thing, matter	(*n.*)	(16)
是	shì	(动)	be, is, are, was, were	(*v.*)	(4)
顺风	shùnfēng		to have a favourable wind	(*v.*)	(15)
送	sòng	(动)	to see off	(*v.*)	(15)
随便	suíbiàn	(形)	as you like, casual	(*adj.*)	(10)

太	tài	(副)	too	(*adv.*)	(15)
谈	tán	(动)	to chat, to talk	(*v.*)	(20)
糖	táng	(名)	sugar, sweets	(*n.*)	(6)
提	tí	(动)	to propose, to make	(*v.*)	(10)
提议	tí yì	(动)	to propose	(*v.*)	(19)
天气	tiānqì	(名)	weather	(*n.*)	(17)
同事	tóngshì	(名)	colleague	(*n.*)	(7)
晚	wǎn	(形)	late	(*adj.*)	(9)
王光	Wáng Guāng	(专名)	name of a person	(*pn.*)	(5)
忘	wàng	(动)	to forget	(*v.*)	(18)
为	wèi	(介)	for	(*prep.*)	(19)
未来	wèilái	(名)	future	(*n.*)	(19)
位	wèi	(量)	(a measure word)	(*mw.*)	(7)
我	wǒ	(代)	I, me	(*pron.*)	(4)
我们	wǒmen	(代)	we	(*pron.*)	(7)
希望	xīwàng	(动)	to hope	(*v.*)	(14)
洗尘	xǐchén	(动)	to give a dinner of welcome to a visitor from afar	(*v.*)	(19)
喜欢	xǐhuan	(动)	to like	(*v.*)	(13)
下	xià	(动)	to go down	(*v.*)	(12)
下	xià	(名)	next	(*n.*)	(17)
下午	xiàwǔ	(名)	afternoon	(*n.*)	(20)
先	xiān	(副)	first	(*adv.*)	(12)
香港	Xiānggǎng	(专名)	Hongkong	(*pn.*)	(20)
想	xiǎng	(动)	to miss	(*v.*)	(14)
销售	xiāoshòu	(动)	to sell	(*v.*)	(7)
小	xiǎo	(形)	young, little	(*adj.*)	(7)
小白	Xiǎo Bái	(专名)	(first name of a person)	(*pn.*)	(7)
小姐	xiǎojiě	(名)	miss	(*n.*)	(4)
效益	xiàoyì	(名)	benefit	(*n.*)	(18)
谢谢	xièxie	(动)	to thank, thanks	(*v.*)	(3)
新	xīn	(形)	new	(*adj.*)	(4)
新来的	xīn lái de		new comer		(4)
新年	xīnnián	(名)	New Year	(*n.*)	(20)

星期	xīngqī	(名)	week	(n.)	(17)
行	xíng	(动)	O.K., fine	(v.)	(10)
行	xíng	(形)	fine	(adj.)	(13)
需要	xūyào	(动)	to need	(v.)	(11)
要	yào	(动)	to want, to need	(v.)	(11)
要	yào	(动)	to be going to	(v.)	(14)
也	yě	(副)	also, too	(adv.)	(5)
一	yī	(数)	a, one	(num.)	(3)
一定	yídìng	(副)	surely	(adv.)	(16)
一路	yílù	(名)	all the way	(n.)	(15)
一起	yìqǐ	(副)	together	(adv.)	(19)
一下	yíxià		for a while		(8)
一直	yìzhí	(副)	continuously	(adv.)	(18)
意见	yìjiàn	(名)	suggestion, comment, complaint	(n.)	(10)
印	yìn	(动)	to print	(v.)	(8)
用	yòng	(动)	need, to use	(v.)	(3)
友谊	yǒuyì	(名)	friendship	(n.)	(19)
愉快	yúkuài	(形)	pleasant	(adj.)	(15)
再	zài	(副)	again	(adv.)	(14)
再见	zàijiàn	(动)	good-bye	(v.)	(14)
在	zài	(介)	at, in, on	(prep.)	(5)
早日	zǎorì	(副)	soon	(adv.)	(14)
怎么样	zěnmeyàng	(代)	How	(pron.)	(17)
照顾	zhàogu	(动)	to take care of	(v.)	(15)
照片	zhàopiàn	(名)	photo	(n.)	(18)
这	zhè	(代)	this	(pron.)	(6)
这个	zhèige		this		(6)
这么	zhème	(副)	such, so	(adv.)	(20)
真	zhēn	(副)	really, awfully	(adv.)	(9)
正	zhèng	(副)	in process of	(adv.)	(18)
中国	Zhōngguó	(专名)	China	(pn.)	(17)
助理	zhùlǐ	(名)	assistant	(n.)	(4)
祝	zhù	(动)	to wish	(v.)	(15)

祝贺	zhùhè	(动)	to congratulate	(*v.*)	(20)
着急	zháojí	(动)	to worry about	(*v.*)	(18)
资料	zīliào	(名)	material	(*n.*)	(9)
自己	zìjǐ	(代)	oneself	(*pron.*)	(12)
总	zǒng	(名)	general, always	(*n.*)	(2)
总部	zǒngbù	(名)	head office, general headquarters	(*n.*)	(8)
走	zǒu	(动)	to go, to walk	(*v.*)	(12)
最近	zuìjìn	(名)	recent	(*n.*)	(17)
坐	zuò	(动)	to sit	(*v.*)	(6)

练习参考答案

Key to the Exercises

第2课

五、1. nǐ hǎo（你好）
2. nǐ hǎo（你好）/ nín hǎo（您好）
3. nǐ hǎo（你好）/ nín hǎo（您好）
4. nǐ hǎo（你好）/ nín hǎo（您好）
5. nín hǎo（您好）
6. nǐmen hǎo（你们好）

第3课

五、1. bú kèqi（不客气）/ bú yòng xiè（不用谢）
2. xièxie nǐ（谢谢你）
3. bú kèqi（不客气）/ bú yòng xiè（不用谢）
4. bú kèqi（不客气）/ bú yòng xiè（不用谢）
5. bú kèqi（不客气）/ bú yòng xiè（不用谢）
6. xièxie nǐ（谢谢你）
7. xièxie nǐmen（谢谢你们）
8. bú kèqi（不客气）/ bú yòng xiè（不用谢）

第4课

五、1. nǐhǎo（你好）
2. wǒmen shì（我们是）
3. xīn lái de（新来的）
4. wǒ shì（我是）
5. xīn lái de（新来的）
6. wǒ shì（我是）

第5课

四、1. ( ) 你 ( ) 是 ( ) 总 经理, ( ) 我 (yě 也) 是 ( ) 总 经理 ( )。
2. ( ) 李琳 ( ) 高兴 ( ), ( ) 刘力 (yě 也) 高兴 ( )。
3. ( ) 麦克 ( ) 在 ( ) 北京 ( ), ( ) John (yě 也) 在 ( ) 北京 ( )。

五、1. huānyíng nǐ（欢迎你）
2. huānyíng nǐmen（欢迎你们）
3. huānyíng guānglín（欢迎光临）

4. huānyíng nǐ（欢迎你）
5. huānyíng （欢迎）
6. huānyíng nǐmen（欢迎你们）

第6课

五、1. xièxie（谢谢）
2. qǐng zuò（请坐）
3. xièxie（谢谢）
4. hē chá（喝茶）
5. xièxie（谢谢）
6. qǐng zuò（请坐）

第7课

四、1. nǐ hǎo（你好）　　nǐ hǎo（你好）
2. wǒ de（我的）　　péngyou（朋友）/ tóngshì（同事）
3. péngyou（朋友）/ tóngshì（同事）
4. nǐ hǎo（你好）

第8课

五、1. kěyǐ（可以）
2. hǎo de（好的）
3. kěyǐ（可以）
4. hǎo de（好的）

第9课

四、1. méi guānxi（没关系）
2. lái wǎn le（来晚了）
3. bàoqiàn（抱歉）
4. duìbuqǐ（对不起）/ bàoqiàn（抱歉）　　méi guānxi（没关系）

五、一（fèn 份）传真
三（tái 台）电脑
五（zhāng 张）纸
七（běn 本）书
六（zhāng 张）桌子

第10课

四、1. kěyǐ（可以）
 2. xíng（行）/ kěyǐ（可以）
 3. diànnǎo（电脑）
 4. xíng（行）/ kěyǐ（可以）

第11课

四、1. bú yòng le（不用了）
 2. bú yòng le（不用了）
 3. bāng máng（帮忙）

五、1. 用我帮忙吗？
 2. 给公司发一个传真。
 3. 我可以不可以用你的电脑？
 4. 咖啡用不用加糖？

第12课

四、1. qǐng（请）
 2. xiān（先）
 3. shàng（上）
 4. qǐng（请）

第13课

四、1. guòjiǎng（过奖）
 2. xíng（行）
 3. zhēn（真）
 4. guòjiǎng（过奖）

第14课

四、1. zàijiàn（再见）
 2. zàijiàn（再见）
 3. zài lái（再来）
 4. zàijiàn（再见）

第15课

四、1. zàijiàn（再见）
　　2. yílù（一路）
　　3. zhù（祝）
　　4. píng'ān（平安）

第16课

四、1. bú kèqi（不客气）
　　2. guò（过）
　　3. qǐng（请）
　　4. xiān（先）

第17课

四、1. máng（忙）
　　2. hǎo（好）
　　3. zěnmeyàng（怎么样）
　　4. hěn hǎo（很好）

第18课

四、1. hǎo（好）
　　2. zháojí（着急）
　　3. bù（不）
　　4. bù（不）

五、1. 不（bú）
　　2. 别（bié）
　　3. 不（bú）
　　4. 不（bù）
　　5. 别（bié）
　　6. 别（bié）

第19课

四、1. gān bēi（干杯）
　　2. xièxie（谢谢）
　　3. yǒuyì（友谊）
　　4. gān bēi（干杯）

五、

今天	5月3日	去年	2004年	星期一	6月20日
昨天	5月2日	今年	2005年	星期六	6月25日
明天	5月4日	明年	2006年	上星期日	6月12日
前天	5月1日	前年	2003年	星期二	6月21日

第20课

四、1．Xièxie（谢谢）
　　2．yě（也）
　　3．kuàilè（快乐）
　　4．Xièxie（谢谢）

五、1．gè wèi（各位）
　　2．gè wèi / dàjiā（各位 / 大家）
　　3．gè wèi（各位）
　　4．gè wèi / dàjiā（各位 / 大家）